# Healthy Crock Pot Meals & other Easy Crock Pot Recipes

Discover over 100 Healthy Crock Pot Recipes, Vegetarian Crock Pot Recipes, Chicken Crock Pot Recipes, Pot Roast Crock Pot Recipes, Beef Stew Recipe, Beef Bourguignon, Beef Stroganoff Recipes, Casserole Recipes, Chili Recipes, Breakfast Casserole Recipes, Dessert Recipes & other Healthy Slow Cooker Recipes

By C Elias

# Contents

|  | Page |
|---|---|
| Introduction | 7 |
| The benefits of using a crock pot | 8 |
| What sort of slow-cooker should you buy? | 9 |
| Getting more specific on features and settings | 12 |
| Essential crock pot cooking tips | 14 |
| Pantry staples for crock pot cooking | 16 |
| Cooking on the fly with a crock pot | 19 |
| Tips for slow cooker soups and stews | 21 |
| Keeping it healthy tips | 24 |
| Crock Pot Chicken | 27 |
|     Simple Barbecue Chicken | 28 |
|     Special Barbecue Chicken | 29 |
|     Simple Chicken Stew | 30 |
|     Quick Cheesy Chicken | 31 |
|     Cheesy Chicken Dinner | 32 |
|     Chicken A La King | 33 |
|     Chicken Cacciatore | 34 |
|     Chicken Casserole | 36 |
|     Tomato and Bean Chicken Casserole | 37 |
|     Special Chicken Stew | 38 |
|     Crusty Chicken Casserole | 40 |
|     Chilli Chicken Dinner | 42 |
|     Chicken Soup | 44 |
|     Country Captain Chicken Breasts | 45 |
|     Cranberry - Apple Turkey Breast | 47 |
|     Creamy Chicken and Rice | 48 |
|     Crock Pot Arroz Con Pollo | 50 |
|     Artichoke, Chicken and Olive Supreme | 51 |
|     Autumn Chicken | 53 |
|     Bourbon Breast of Chicken | 54 |
|     Cream Cheese Chicken Crock | 56 |
|     Braised Chicken Curry with Yams | 57 |
|     Brown Rice and Chicken | 58 |
|     Cafe Chicken | 59 |
|     Carrot Chicken | 61 |
|     Chicken A La King | 63 |

| | |
|---|---|
| Quick Chicken and Noodles | 64 |
| Chicken and Turkey Sausage Paella | 65 |
| Chicken Cacciatore | 67 |
| Extra Rich Chicken Cacciatore | 68 |
| Chicken Cordon Bleu | 70 |
| Simple Chicken in a Pot | 71 |
| Chicken Noodle Soup | 72 |
| Traditional Chicken Stew | 73 |
| Mexican Chicken Stew | 74 |
| Coq au vin | 75 |
| Burgundy coq au vin | 77 |
| Fiesta Chicken | 78 |
| Garlic Chicken with Cabbage | 79 |
| Greek Chicken | 80 |
| Jerk Chicken | 81 |
| Lazy Crock Pot Chicken | 82 |
| Lemon Rosemary Chicken | 83 |
| Lo-Cal Crock Pot Chicken | 84 |
| Low-Fat Chicken and Veggie Bake | 85 |
| Mediterranean Style Chicken | 86 |
| Creamy Chicken and Broccoli | 87 |
| Angel Pasta Chicken | 89 |
| Little Italy Chicken and Spinach Lasagna | 90 |
| Sweet Cranberry Chicken | 92 |
| Lemon Pucker Chicken | 93 |
| Overnight Spicy Roasted Chicken | 94 |
| Squash Chicken | 95 |
| Honey Me Up Chicken | 96 |
| Spicy Chicken Wings Appetizer | 97 |
| **Crock Pot Beans** | **98** |
| Mixed Bean Soup | 99 |
| Barbecued Bean Soup | 101 |
| Black Bean Chili | 102 |
| Black Bean Soup | 104 |
| White Bean Soup | 105 |
| Aztec Black Beans | 106 |
| Baked Beans Supreme | 107 |
| Black Bean Chili Soup | 108 |
| Black Eyed Peas | 109 |

| | |
|---|---:|
| Crock Pot Beef | 110 |
|     All Day Crock Pot Beef | 111 |
|     Barbeque Beef Stew | 112 |
|     Barbecue Steak | 113 |
|     Beer Meatballs | 114 |
|     Chili Beef Dinner | 116 |
|     Late Breakfast or Brunch Casserole | 117 |
|     Beef and Beans Lunch | 119 |
|     Winter 4 Bean Chili | 120 |
|     Black Bean Chili | 121 |
|     Beef Bourguignon | 122 |
|     Beef Burger Stroganoff | 123 |
|     Beef Burgundy | 124 |
|     Beef Fajitas | 125 |
|     Beef n Brew Vegetable Soup | 127 |
|     Beef Pot Roast | 128 |
|     Beef Stew | 129 |
|     Quick Beef Stew | 130 |
|     Beef Stroganoff | 131 |
|     Quick Beef Stroganoff | 132 |
|     Beef Taco Bean Soup | 133 |
|     Black Bean & Beef Chili | 134 |
|     Cabbage and Beef Casserole | 135 |
|     Carne Gisada | 136 |
|     Hamburger Chili | 137 |
|     Quick Chili | 138 |
|     Chili Con Carne | 139 |
|     Greek Stew | 140 |
|     Mexican Chili | 141 |
| Crock Pot Vegetables | 142 |
|     Asparagus Casserole | 143 |
|     Broccoli and Cheese Soup | 144 |
|     Creamy Scalloped Potatoes | 145 |
|     Crock Pot Artichokes | 146 |
|     Crock Pot Caponata | 147 |
|     Green Bean & Potato Casserole | 148 |
|     Bavarian Red Cabbage | 149 |
|     Cheese & Potato Casserole | 150 |
|     Cheese & Artichoke Dip | 151 |

|  |  |
|---|---|
| Cheesy Cauliflower & Broccoli | 152 |
| Broccoli Soup | 153 |
| Corn Chowder | 154 |
| Creamy Spinach Noodle Casserole | 155 |
| Potato Soup | 156 |
| Spaghetti Squash | 157 |
| Vegetable Casserole | 158 |
| Vegetable Curry | 161 |
| Vegetable Pasta | 162 |
| Vegetables Italian Style | 163 |
| Zucchini Casserole | 165 |
| Crock Pot Miscellaneous | 166 |
| Barley with Mushrooms & Green Onions | 167 |
| Classic Swiss Fondue | 168 |
| All Day Macaroni Cheese | 170 |
| No Eggs Macaroni Cheese | 171 |
| Baked Potatoes | 172 |
| Banana Bread | 173 |
| Banana Nut Bread | 175 |
| Cajun Pecans | 177 |
| Chunky Applesauce | 178 |
| Breakfast Casserole | 179 |
| Cranapple Sauce | 180 |
| Crock Pot Fish | 181 |
| Citrus Fish | 182 |
| Fish in Tomato Sauce | 183 |
| Crock Pot Desserts | 184 |
| Apple Cranberry Compote | 185 |
| Apple Cranberry Crisp | 186 |
| Baked Apples | 187 |
| Breakfast Cobbler | 188 |
| Carrot Pudding | 189 |
| Christmas Bread Pudding | 190 |
| Apple Sauce | 193 |
| Conclusion | 194 |

Legal Notice:

The author and publisher of this book have used their best efforts in preparing this book. The author and publisher make no representation or warranties with respect to the accuracy, applicability, or completeness of the contents of this book. The information contained in this book is strictly for educational purposes. Therefore, if you wish to apply ideas contained in this book, you are taking full responsibility for your actions.
The author and publisher disclaim any warranties (express or implied), merchantability, for any particular purpose. The author and publisher shall in no event be held liable to any party for any direct, indirect, punitive, special, incidental or other consequential damages arising directly or indirectly from any use of this material, which is provided "as is", and without warranties.

## Introduction

In these modern times, families are always very busy. Everyone's schedule is tight – from parents down to the youngest child. So fitting in a good home-cooked meal can be hard. But help is at hand - the "slow cooker"!

It provides families with another way to prepare delicious meals for their household. The best part is that you don't even have to be there while it's cooking.

Slow cooker is another way to say "crock pot." Most of us are used to hearing the latter, but the terms are interchangeable meaning the same thing.

The term "slow cooker" means a counter-top appliance which has an heating element and heat proof dish (crock) housed in an outer case and a lid - it is designed to cook foods by slow, moist heat. Crock-Pot™ is the brand name of a particular manufacturer but has become the nick-name if you like for slow cookers.

You can cook with a 'crock pot' designed for the stove or oven as well. The recipes herein are for table top crock pots but you can use the other variety if you wish.

## The benefits of using a crock pot

So why would you want to use a slow cooker? What's the point of cooking at a lower temperature?

- ✔ You save money on energy as they require very little power to operate.
- ✔ You have a cooler kitchen due to the lower energy used.
- ✔ You can use tougher cuts of meat as the slow and long cooking time ensures the collagen in the connective tissue is broken down resulting in tender succulent meat.
- ✔ It is convenient as the ingredients can be prepared at a time of your choosing - either the night before or in the morning - then placed in the crock ready for cooking slowly.
- ✔ You only need one pot for to cook a meal.
- ✔ It's healthier to cook meat and vegetables at lower temperatures.

## What sort of a Slow Cooker you should buy

You can get crock pots in various sizes. Select a slow cooker which suits your family needs. A 3.5 litre (which translates as a usable volume of 2 litres) will feed two to four people and a 6 litre one (which you can fill with 4.5 litres) will feed six to eight people.

Choose a round shape if you think you will mainly be cooking recipes such as stews or curries. Pick an oval shape if you feel you may wish to cook whole joints or poultry.

Outer Housing Unit:

The base should be sturdy and allow air to flow underneath and dissipate heat. Choosing a cool-wall unit is also advisable.

The inner Crock:

A removable crock is far easier to clean and use, and allows for refrigeration of foods before and after cooking. It also is great for serving the food in – just put it on the table and everyone can help themselves.

As a full crock can be heavy, solid handles are a must. Also, bear in mind that a heavier crock will better withstand accidental bumps when moving (from fridge to housing unit), serving, washing up and storage.

Lid:

A glass lid is the best option. If you think you will be cooking joints of meat or whole poultry, a higher domed lid is a good choice as it will allow more room for cooking taller foods.

Most slow cookers also come with removable inner pots that allow for easier serving at the dinner table. A removable inner core allows everyone to sit and relax as they spoon their food onto the plate instead of standing at the stove. It is also much easier to clean!

Make sure the crock is ceramic. I am not an expert on materials used in cookware, but ceramic seems to be the safest material for baking and cooking (see mercola.com). Sometimes there are non-stick crock pots available which I would be wary of. This is because non-stick bake ware is made from perfluorooctanoic acid (PFOA), a synthetic chemical used in production that creates the slipperiness and non-stick finish. When heated this non-stick bake ware can reach temperatures at which toxic fumes are released.

Apparently the coating begins to break down and release toxins at a temperature of only 446°F. PFOA has become controversial because of potential health dangers...

So, although slow cookers generally don't go above 300°F, I would personally still be on the safe side and *avoid* anything "non-stick".

## Temperature settings:

Temperature settings vary among slow cookers. Many offer a range of temperature settings to meet the needs of the cook. Some have as little at two settings (high and low) and others include five settings that vary from high (two hours) to really slow cooking (ten hours).

In general, slow cookers heat the contents of the crock to 160C/300°F with the food never reaching 100C/212F i.e. boiling point. Because of this low temperature, food can be cooked for a long time without risk of burning. These low cooking temperatures also mean it is safe to leave the slow cooker unattended. Furthermore if the food is left for longer than the stated time, it generally does not overcook.

There may also be a warm setting in case the food has finished cooking but any accompanying side dishes still need to be prepared. This setting is also great for times when everyone isn't ready to eat their meal just yet.

When you get your slow cooker you may prefer to test it first to see how quickly food will cook on the different settings. So don't wait until you have a dinner party! Use your family to test on!

## Getting more specific on features and settings:

Auto cook -

This starts the crock pot on high and after an hour continues to cook on low. Although not all models have this function, apparently a lot of people think the best results are achieved using this particular setting.

Low setting -

This setting is good for cooking cheaper cuts of red meats. In general, cooking on this setting vary between 8 to 12 hours.

Hi (high) setting -

This is recommended for cooking white meats such as chicken. Generally, this setting cooks for 3 to 6 hours at a slightly higher temperature.

Med (medium) setting -

This setting is used when faster cooking is needed but without losing all the slow cooking benefits. Some models don't have this though.

Keep warm setting

This setting is used purely to keep finished recipes from drying out if you are delayed, but stops it getting cold.

Timer -

Timers can be used to turn the setting 'keep warm' after the meals is cooked. However, not all models have a timer so if you are at work most days and need this extra time at the end of the cooking, then make sure you get one with a timer.

On indicator light -

It's useful to have an indicator light to show when your cooker is on.

**Essential Crock Pot Cooking Tips**

1. What you must remember when cooking anything in a slow cooker is the liquid component. There must be some type of liquid in the bottom of the cooker to begin the cooking process. Without it, your dish will cook to the bottom and burn. There doesn't need to be a lot of it, just enough to cover the bottom in most cases. The juices within the meat will mingle with the other liquid during cooking to create more of a stock.

2. When using a crock pot it should be at least half full for maximum cooking potential. Keep in mind that the more food you add to the cooker, the slower it will cook. The temperature will cook the food evenly without overcooking if the heat settings are adjusted accordingly. If you aren't careful and don't adjust the crock pot heat settings, you may find that an eight hour setting cooked your dinner in two and spent the other six drying it out!

3. Meats are the most common food cooked in a slow cooker. People use a crock pot to cook main dishes for dinner since this is the meal we struggle with preparing most on a busy schedule. Any meat used needs to be thoroughly drained before adding it to the cooker. Since meat takes longer to cook, they need to make up the bottom layer. This will also help keep the meat moist since it will cook into the liquid underneath.

4. For safety, cook meats at least three hours so that an internal temperature that is high enough for proper cooking can be reached.
5. If you plan to cook vegetables in your slow cooker, here are some tips. Tough fibrous veggies like carrots and potatoes can be tossed in at the beginning with the meat. It takes longer for the fibers to be broken down and the vegetables to be cooked all the way through. More delicate vegetables like tomatoes, peppers, and mushrooms should be added half an hour before the meal is done.
6. Slow cooking makes dinner a cinch when you are on the run. Just be sure to experiment with various dishes the first time to get an idea of how long your slow cooker takes to create the particular meal. Layering foods correctly and testing heat settings will ensure your meal will be delicious every time.

## Pantry Staples for Crock Pot Cooking

A slow cooker in the kitchen will pay for itself in no time. The time it saves when preparing meals makes it priceless. But, if you plan on using your slow cooker quite often, there are a few staples you may want to keep on hand to enhance your dishes.

1. Beans – Beans are a cheap source of protein that cook well. Each bean has its own flavor which is enhanced by the spices you use to cook them. Beans can be used as a meal base when meat is present or if you are a vegetarian looking to create an easy dish without much fuss. Whether navy, lentil, Northern, or black, beans create some amazing slow cooker meals.

2. Fibrous Vegetables – The average household has at least a few potatoes lurking around. They are a versatile food. Mash them, fry them, stew them, or throw them in the crock pot. Potatoes add density to soups, stews, and meals with meat. Because they, and other fibrous veggies like turnips and carrots, take longer to cook, they can be thrown in the cooker with the meat and allowed to cook all day.

3. Fresh Herbs – Herbs can dramatically change the flavor of almost any meal. Herbs come dried, but release a better flavor if they are fresh. You can grow your own herbs in the house in small pots. All you need is a sunny spot, good soil, and water. Home

grown herbs can be dried to extend their life, making them easy to keep around without worrying about wasting them. Herbs are added near the end of the crock pot cooking cycle so their flavor infiltrates the cooked meal.

4. Broth – Anything cooked in the slow cooker needs a liquid to start the process. Instead of always adding water, try broth. Chicken, beef, and vegetable broth are available in most grocery stores for very little money. Many varieties come already seasoned and it's a quick and easy way to add flavor to meat dishes.

5. Flour – Flour, cornstarch, gluten-free flours etc. are used for thickening and sautéing. Applying a light coating of flour to meats and sautéing them in a little olive oil will create flavorful bits of essence that can be added to the slow cooker. At the end of a meal, adding cornstarch to the remaining liquid can create creamy gravy for dishes like rice or potatoes. Flour can also be used as a thickener, however cornstarch makes smoother gravies.

6. Meat – This article is about pantry staples, but since meat is the centerpiece of most crock pot meals, be sure to have some of your favorites on hand (in the freezer of course). It can be any meat you choose. A tougher cut of meat will cook better and almost melt in your mouth when the dish is ready. Slow cooking will add moisture and tenderize meat that would

otherwise dry out and be tough when cooked in the oven.

With these ingredients on hand, you can create any number of basic meals in the slow cooker. By keeping them on hand, you'll have a variety of dinner ideas without the hassle of running to the store or searching for an answer when asked "What's for dinner?"

## Cooking on the Fly with a Crock Pot

If you have an adventurous cooking spirit or would like to and a cabinet or pantry full of goodies, it's easy to create a slow cooker meal from scratch. I know you are shaking your head, but it is doable and your family will love it. In fact, why not let everyone get in on the meal to make it more interesting?

When putting together a potluck slow cooker meal, you need a base or main ingredient. Meat or beans make the perfect base. Although grains also make a good base for meals, they cook too quickly to be of any use to you in a slow cooker. Rice quickly becomes mushy when it is overcooked and pastas work best when boiled. Therefore, slow cooking these types of foods would potentially ruin them.

Your base is something that can stand up to the length of time required for crock pot cooking and the temperature. Chicken, turkey, beef, lamb, pork etc are all good choices for a meat base. Most beans can stand up to the heating process of a slow cooker. Once you have made a choice for your meal base, wash it thoroughly and put it in the cooker. Don't forget to add a bit of liquid to the bottom first.

The next step is to decide what will go well with the base chosen. Most meat types share the fact that they are compatible with many of the same vegetables. First, check the fridge. A bag of baby carrots, an onion, and some celery are staring you in the face. These we can use. Go ahead and toss the carrots right in on top of your meat or bean base.

Now start the cooker while you search for more ingredients. See that bag of red-skinned potatoes in the corner? The best thing about them is that they don't have to be peeled. Simply, wash the outer skin thoroughly and pop them into the cooker as well. No need to slice or dice them beforehand.

Remember that celery and onion from your refrigerator? Throw them in a skillet with salt, pepper, and cooking wine if you have it. Let the wine reduce and cook the veggies.

Now it's time to think about spices and seasonings. What will go well with your base? For kick, add some turmeric, cumin, and cilantro. Curry goes well with chicken or pork for a more Indian flavor. On the Italian side, choose rosemary, basil, oregano, bay leaf, and coriander. Remember, fresh herbs have a more distinctive taste than powdered spices, so if you have some on hand, use those instead.

About an hour before the end of the cooking time, add your sautéed veggies and spices. Stir and smell the wonderful flavor. If there is still too much liquid left for your liking, turn the cooker up on high and remove the lid. The liquid will evaporate and you can return to low after the desired level of broth is achieved.

## Tips for Slow Cooked Soups and Stews

It seems like the slow cooker was practically made for soups and stews. On a cold fall or winter day, you can combine the ingredients for your favorite soup in the pot and fill the house with a delicious aroma while it cooks. Everyone needs to make at least one soup or stew in their slow cooker!

Why do we like soups? They are fun and easy to make. Many cultures rely on soup as their main dish for lunch or dinner. A soup can be thin like chicken noodle or some Thai soups. A soup can also be thick like vichyssoise or borscht (Ukrainian soup usually made with beets and starchy veg) which represents ethnic soup dishes. Thicker soups keep you full longer between meals. Add a bit of bread and you have a complete meal.

Soups require more liquid than a regular meal in a slow cooker. Don't be afraid to add two or three cups of broth or water to your cooker when creating soup dishes. If you have a larger slow cooker, you may need to add a bit more liquid depending on how many other ingredients you also add.

If your main ingredient is meat, add it first. For soups it is a good idea to cut raw chicken into small cubes. For beef, buy already cubed beef for stew to avoid having to cube it yourself. Meat should be thawed for soups and stews before adding to the crock pot. You can sear (cooking the outside in a pan until crusty leaving the inside still uncooked) meats in a pan before adding them to the cooker. A bit of water will remove those pieces of essence from the bottom of the skillet so they can be added to the soup for flavor.

Go ahead and add your vegetables to the soup once the meat has been put in. Chop potatoes, carrots, squash, zucchini, and onions into soup-sized pieces. Frozen veggies can also be added to the soup. Let your soup concoction cook for six to eight hours. Celery is a common veggie in soups. For a firmer celery texture, wait to add the celery until a couple of hours before the end of cooking.

Creamier soups are also a good choice for slow cooker meals. Heavy cream can stand up to the longer cooking time without scorching. If milk is called for in your dish, use evaporated milk in its place. Evaporated milk has had the water component removed and provides a creamier texture without the curdling effect that can be common when using straight milk.

Now you are ready to add the finishing touches. When making soups like potato soup or chowders that call for cheese, wait until close to done before adding the cheese. Herbs like rosemary, dill, basil, oregano, and parsley can be added now too. Chives, leeks, shallots, and garlic also add flavor to soups and stews. Chives, parsley, and leeks can be used as a garnish.

Can you taste that soup now? The best thing about soup is that it can be frozen in bowls and thawed whenever you feel like some warm-in-your-tummy goodness. A slow cooker makes a batch large enough to feed an army or a large family of hungry eaters.

Also the soups you make can be kept frozen and used for other crock pot recipes.

## Keeping it Healthy Tips

As the owner of a fitness and weight loss site www.effective-diets.com, an ezinearticles.com expert in Health and Fitness and a regular health researcher to keep up to date with the healthiest foods, new super-foods, the foods to avoid and so on, I feel it is my duty to include here a little on what I have discovered and know about certain foods, to help my readers make informed choices. For more information do check out my book *Healthy Eating Tips* on Amazon.

## Sugar

Most recipes these days add a little sugar for a touch of sweetness. Sugar, however, is now being recognized as one of the worst foods we could possibly eat. In a nutshell, it plays havoc with your insulin levels – insulin is released by your pancreas to normalize your blood sugar levels. Eating sugar regularly causes 'insulin resistance' in the cells of the body, which is now considered by some experts as the main cause of obesity, fatigue, high blood pressure, heart disease, diabetes, dementia, Alzheimer's, and several cancers.

To avoid all this, use a natural sweetener. Do not use any artificial sweetener. These are also very bad for your health.

Use *xylitol* – a natural sweetener you can probably find in your local health shop or online, which is found in fruit and vegetables, birch and hardwood trees. This has a low GI, is anti-bacterial, does not cause blood sugar level fluctuations or need insulin to be metabolized. (Don't give food made with xylitol to your pets though – it has a different effect on their bodies and can cause serious problems)

Alternatively, you can use *stevia* powder or liquid. Stevia is a very sweet herb used for 1500 years in South America and has virtually no calories – it is the safest sweetener on the market.

## Pork

Considered by many as dirty due to the eating habits of pigs, it does harbor parasites which are difficult to kill in cooking. Getting sick from eating dirty pork is more common than you think and pigs also harbor viruses – organic pork is not safe either - because pigs don't sweat and the way it digests food quickly – toxins stay in their meat rather than get flushed away.

So it's your choice but there are plenty of other meats you can eat in place of pork – and for that reason, (at the expense of possibly losing a few readers), I have not included a section for crock pot pork although of course you can substitute pork into most of the meat recipes if you wish. I hope that if you love eating other meat, beans and veg you will find this book very useful and satisfying!

## Other Meat

I thoroughly recommend you cook with free range or organic chicken and grass fed beef if you are able to. Not only is the taste better but you are doing your body and everyone else's a favor. With less toxins, hormones and chemicals in the meat, you can really enjoy your crock pots!

## Sauces

When the recipes included here call for already made sauces and soup packets etc, then try and find organic ones or at least ones with no additives or sugar – alternatively you can make your own sauces, soups or broths for the recipes or use another ingredient such as tomato puree instead of sauce but add some herbs and maybe a touch of stevia or xylitol.

Do experiment with your cooking – you may find a recipe needs a little extra something anyway – don't be afraid to add more ingredients!

# Crock Pot Chicken

## SIMPLE BARBECUE CHICKEN

Ingredients:

1 Chicken, cut up and skin removed

1 cup ketchup (or 3/4 cup brown sugar)

3 tablespoons Worcestershire sauce

Directions:

Place chicken in crock pot.

Combine remaining ingredients and pour over chicken.

Cook 4 hours on high or 8-10 hours on low.

## SPECIAL BARBECUE CHICKEN

Ingredients:
4-6 pieces chicken (boneless breasts)
1 bottle BBQ sauce
½ cup white vinegar
½ cup brown sugar (or xylitol)
1 tsp. mesquite seasoning
½ tsp. garlic powder
½-1 tsp. red pepper flakes

Directions:
Mix BBQ sauce with all ingredients listed under it.
Place chicken in crock pot.
Pour sauce over all.
Cook slowly in crock pot about 5 - 6 hours.
Serve with baked beans, potato salad and coleslaw.

## SIMPLE CHICKEN STEW

Ingredients:

1 chicken, 3 lbs, cut up

2 quarts Water

1 onion, chopped

3 potatoes, diced

2 cans tomatoes; cut up

10 ounces lima beans, frozen and thawed

10 ounces corn; whole kernel, frozen, partially thawed

2 teaspoons salt

1 teaspoon sugar to suit (use xylitol or stevia)

¼ teaspoon pepper

½ teaspoon seasoned salt

Directions:

In a Crock Pot combine chicken with water, onion, and potatoes. Cook covered on LOW for 4 to 5 hours or until chicken is done. Lift chicken out of pot; remove meat from bones. Return chicken meat to pot.

Add tomatoes, beans, corn, salt, seasoned salt, sugar and pepper. Cover and Cook on HIGH 1 hour.

Makes 8 servings.

## QUICK CHEESY CHICKEN

Ingredients:

3 whole boneless chicken breasts

2 cans cream chicken soup (see soup recipes if you want to make yourself)

1 can cheddar cheese soup (see soup recipes if you want to make this yourself)

Directions:

Remove all fat and skin from chicken;

rinse and pat dry, sprinkle with salt, pepper and garlic powder.

Put in crock pot and add the three soups straight from the cans.

Cook on low all day (at least 8 hrs) do not lift the lid.

Serve over rice or noodles.

## CHEESY CHICKEN DINNER

Ingredients:

6 chicken breasts (boneless & skinless)

salt & pepper to taste

garlic powder, to taste

2 cans cream of chicken soup (or make your own)

1 can cheddar cheese soup (or make your own)

Directions:

Rinse chicken and sprinkle with salt, pepper and garlic powder.

Mix the soups together then pour over chicken in the crock pot. Cook on low 6 to 8 hours.

Serve over rice or noodles.

## CHICKEN A LA KING

Ingredients:

1½ to 2 pounds boneless chicken tenders

1 to 1½ cup matchstick-cut carrots

1 bunch green onions (scallions) sliced in 1/2-inch pieces

1 to 1½ cup of olive and cheese spread (or make yourself – see below)

1 can 98% fat-free cream of chicken soup

2 tablespoons dry sherry (optional)

salt and pepper to taste

Directions:

Put all ingredients in the slow cooker/Crock Pot (3½ -quart or larger) in the order given;

stir to combine.

Cover and cook on low for 7 to 9 hours.

Serve over rice, toast, or biscuits.

Serves 6 to 8.

Olive and cheese spread recipe:

Ingredients:

1 c. Non-fat cream cheese

1/2 tsp Dry basil

¼ tsp garlic powder

15 x Black olives, minced

¼ c. Pimientos, diced

1 tbsp. Minced fresh chives

Directions:

Just mix the seasonings with the cream cheese and then stir in the olives and pimientos.

## CHICKEN CACCIATORE

Ingredients:

Chicken pieces

1 Can of chopped tomatoes

1 chopped onion

1 chopped green pepper

1 minced garlic clove

1 tbsp of Italian herbs

Red pepper flakes

Black olives and mushrooms optional

Directions:

Place cut up chicken in crock pot, cover with tomatoes, and the rest of the ingredients.

You can add mushrooms too if you wish.

Cook all on low 6-8 hours until falling apart. Pop in the olives in the last hour.

Serve over pasta, sprinkling more pepper flakes and Parmesan cheese.

# CHICKEN CASSEROLE

Ingredients:

1 8oz pkg noodles

3 cups diced cooked chicken

½ cup diced celery

½ cup diced green pepper

½ cup diced onion

1 x 4 oz can mushrooms

1 x 4 oz jar pimiento

½ cup parmesan cheese

1½ cups cream style cottage cheese

1 cup grated cheese

1 can cream of chicken soup

½ cup chicken broth

2 tbsp. melted butter

½ tsp. basil

Directions:

Cook noodles according to pkg directions and drain and rinse thoroughly.

In a large bowl, combine remaining ingredients with noodles until well mixed. Pour mixture into greased crock pot. Cover and cook on low for 6-8 hours or high 3-4 hours. Serves 6

# TOMATO AND BEAN CHICKEN CASSEROLE

Ingredients:

2 whole chicken breasts, skinned, deboned, cut in ½" chunks

Celery heart

1 med. onion

2 cans chopped tomatoes, sliced

16 oz med. salsa or picante sauce

1 can chick peas (or 1 pkg. white kidney beans)

6 oz mushrooms

Olive oil or coconut oil

Directions:

Brown chicken in 1 tablespoon oil.

Chop celery, onion and mushrooms.

Combine all ingredients in large crock pot, stir and simmer on low heat for 6-8 hours.

Serve with bread or taco chips.

If you like it spicy, use hot salsa or picante sauce.

## SPECIAL CHICKEN STEW

Ingredients:

2½ to 3 lbs. chicken pieces, skinned

3 cups sliced fresh mushrooms

1 large onion, chopped

2 cloves garlic, minced

¾ cup chicken broth

1 x 6oz can tomato paste

¼ cup dry red wine (such as Merlot) or chicken broth

2 tbsp. quick-cooking tapioca

2 tbsp. snipped fresh basil or 1 ½ tsp. dried basil, crushed (I used dried)

2 tsp. Sugar (stevia or xylitol) optional

¼ tsp. salt

¼ tsp. pepper

2 c. hot cooked noodles

2 tbsp. finely shredded Parmesan cheese

Directions:

Rinse chicken; set aside.

In crock pot place mushrooms, onion, and garlic.

Place chicken pieces on top of the vegetables.

In a bowl combine broth, tomato paste, wine or chicken broth, tapioca, dried basil (if using), sugar (if using), salt, and pepper.

Pour over all. Cover; cook on low-heat setting for 7 to 8 hours or on high-heat setting for 3½ to 4 hours.

If using, stir in fresh basil.

To serve, spoon chicken, mushroom mixture, and sauce over hot cooked noodles.

Sprinkle with Parmesan cheese.

Makes 4 to 6 servings.

## CRUSTY CHICKEN CASSEROLE

Ingredients:

3 cups diced cooked chicken or turkey

2 cans (14½oz each) chicken broth

½ teaspoon salt

½ teaspoon pepper

1 stalk celery, thinly sliced

1 medium onion, chopped

1 bay leaf

3 cups potatoes, peeled and cubed

1 package frozen mixed veggies (16oz)

1 cup milk (any type of milk to suit)

1 cup flour (plain flour, gluten-free flour etc)

1 teaspoon pepper

½ teaspoon salt

1 x 9-inch refrigerated pie crust

Directions:

In Crock Pot, combine chicken, broth, salt, pepper, celery, onion, bay leaf, potatoes, and mixed vegetables.

Cover and cook on low 8 to 10 hours or on high 4 to 6 hours.

Remove bay leaf.

Pre heat oven to 400 degrees F.

In a small bowl, mix milk and flour. (If you want to experiment with oat milk or almond milk etc. then take a bit of the mixture in the crock pot out and mix in your choice of flour and milk and judge the results)

Gradually stir flour and water mixture into Crock Pot.

Stir in pepper, poultry seasoning, and salt.

Remove the liner from Crock Pot base and carefully place 9-inch pie crust over the mixture.

Place the crockery liner inside preheated oven and bake (uncovered) for about 15 minutes, or until browned.

If your liner is not removable, put the mixture in another casserole dish, cover with the pie crust and bake as above.

Serves 8.

## CHILI CHICKEN DINNER

Ingredients:

3 whole chicken breasts (1½ to 2 lbs, cut in 1 inch pieces)

1 cup chopped onion

1 cup chopped bell pepper

2 garlic cloves

2 tbsp. vegetable oil

2 cans Mexican stewed tomatoes (16 ounce each)

1 can chili beans

2/3 cup picante sauce (you can make your own – see below)

1 teaspoon. chili powder

1 teaspoon. cumin

½ teaspoon. Salt

Directions:

Saute chicken, onion, pepper, garlic in vegetable oil until vegetables are wilted.

Transfer to crock pot and add remaining ingredients.

Cook, covered, on low, for 4 to 6 hours.

Serve over rice.

Serves 4 to 6.

Your own picante sauce - In a sauce pan mix the following:

1 can tomato puree
2 tbsp White Vinegar
1/3 cup Onion finely chopped
3 Jalapeño peppers chopped fine
½ tsp Salt
1 - ¼ cup water
Bring content to boil.
Reduce heat and simmer until thick.
Remove from heat and allow to cool.
Place in jars for storage.

## CHICKEN SOUP

Ingredients:

2 onions, chopped

3 carrots, sliced

2 stalks celery, sliced

2 teaspoons salt

¼ teaspoon pepper

½ teaspoon basil

¼ teaspoon leaf thyme

3 tablespoons dry parsley flakes

1 package frozen peas (10 oz)

About 3 lb. chicken meat

4 cups water or chicken stock

1 cup noodles

Directions:

Place all ingredients in crock pot, except noodles, in order listed.

Cover and cook on low 8 to 10 hours, or high 4 to 6 hours.

One hour before serving, remove chicken and cool slightly.

Remove meat from bones and return meat to slow crock pot.

Add noodles. Turn to high. Cover and cook 1 hour.

# COUNTRY CAPTAIN CHICKEN BREASTS

Ingredients:

2 medium-size Granny Smith apples

1 small onion, finely chopped

1 small green bell pepper, seeded and finely chopped

3 cloves garlic, minced or pressed

2 tablespoons dried currants

1 tablespoon curry powder

1 teaspoon ground ginger

¼ teaspoon ground red pepper (cayenne)

1 can (about 14 ½ oz) diced tomatoes

6 small skinless, boneless chicken breast halves (about 1 ¾ lbs. total)

½ cup chicken broth

1 cup long-grain white rice

1 pound large raw shrimp (optional), shelled and deveined

1/3 cup slivered almonds

Salt

Chopped parsley

Directions:

Quarter, core, and dice unpeeled apples.

In a 4-quart or larger crock pot, combine apples, onion, bell pepper, garlic, currants, curry powder, ginger, and red pepper. Stir in tomatoes.

Rinse chicken and pat dry

Then arrange, overlapping pieces slightly, on top of tomato mixture.

Pour in broth.

Cover and cook at low setting until chicken is very tender when pierced (6 to 7 hours).

Carefully lift chicken to a warm plate, cover lightly, and keep warm in a 200 degree oven.

Stir rice into cooking liquid. Increase cooker heat setting to high.

Cover and cook, stirring once or twice, until rice is almost tender to bite (30 to 35 minutes).

Stir in shrimp, cover and cook until shrimp are opaque in center; cut to test (about 10 more minutes).

Meanwhile, toast almonds in a small nonstick frying pan over medium heat until golden brown (5 to 8 minutes), stirring occasionally. Set aside.

To serve, season rice mixture to taste with salt.

Mound in a warm serving dish; arrange chicken on top.

Sprinkle with parsley and almonds.

Makes 6 servings.

## CRANBERRY-APPLE TURKEY BREAST

Ingredients:

2 teaspoons melted butter or margarine

½ cup chicken broth

1 large apple, cored and chopped

½ cup chopped onion

1 stalk celery, chopped

1 cup whole berry cranberry sauce

¾ teaspoon poultry seasoning

2 cups seasoned crumb-style stuffing

2 to 3 pounds turkey breast cutlets.

Directions:

Combine butter, chicken broth, apple, onion, celery, cranberry sauce, poultry seasoning and stuffing.

Place 3 tablespoons stuffing mix on each turkey cutlet.

Roll up and tie.

Place in stoneware.

Cover and cook on low 8 hours (high 4 hours).

## CREAMY CHICKEN AND RICE

Ingredients:

Chicken tenders or breasts

Cream of mushroom soup

(1 can for 2-3 people, 2 for 4-6)

Onion Soup Mix (1 per each can of soup)

1tbsp olive oil

Long grain brown rice (1 cup per can of soup)

1 tbsp whole thyme, crushed

Salt & Pepper to taste

Your desired amount of broccoli florets (optional)

Diced red pepper (optional)

Directions:

When using brown rice, you need 2¼ cups liquid for each 1 cup rice.

Empty can of soup into a measuring cup, and add water (or white wine) to equal 2½ (you need the extra for the onion soup mix).

Heat olive oil in a saute pan, and add rice until it begins to crackle, but not brown.

This will make the rice dense, and help it keep it's shape while cooking.

Whisk together the soups and additional water, herbs and seasonings.

Combine all ingredients (except veggies) in crock pot, and cook on high 4-6 hours, or 8-10 hours on low.

During last 30-45 minutes, add desired veggies.

Great with crusty bread, and a fresh salad.

## CROCK POT ARROZ CON POLLO

Ingredients:
4 Chicken breast halves, skin and excess fat removed
¼ teaspoon salt
¼ tsp pepper
¼ teaspoon paprika
1 tablespoon oil
1 medium onion, chopped
1 small red pepper, chopped
1 clove of garlic, minced
½ teaspoon dried rosemary leaves
1 x 14 ½ ounce can crushed tomatoes
1 x 10 oz package frozen peas

Directions
Season chicken with salt, pepper, and paprika.
In a medium skillet, heat oil over medium-high heat.
Add chicken and brown. Put chicken in the Crock-pot.
In a small bowl, combine remaining ingredients except the peas.
Pour over chicken. Cover: cook on Low 7-9 hours (High 3-4 hours).
One hour before serving, add peas.
Serve over rice. Makes 4 servings.

# ARTICHOKE, CHICKEN AND OLIVE SUPREME

Ingredients:

1 ½lbs skinless, boneless chicken breast halves and/or thighs

2 c. sliced fresh mushrooms

1 (14.5 oz) can diced tomatoes

1 (8 or 9 oz) pkg frozen artichokes

1 c. chicken broth

1 med onion, chopped

½c. sliced pitted ripe olives (or 1/4 cup capers, drained)

¼ c. dry white wine or chicken broth

3 tbsp quick cooking tapioca

2-3 tsp curry powder

¾ tsp dried thyme, crushed

¼ tsp salt

¼ tsp pepper

4 c. hot cooked couscous

Directions:

Rinse chicken & set aside.

In a 3½ qt crock pot combine mushrooms, undrained, tomatoes, frozen artichoke hearts, chicken broth, onion, olives, & wine/broth.

Stir in tapioca, curry powder, thyme, salt, & pepper.

Add chicken.

Spoon some of the tomato mixture over chicken.

Cover & cook on low for 7 to 8 hours or on high for 3 1/2 to 4 hours.

Serve with hot cooked couscous or other.

Serves 6.

## AUTUMN CHICKEN

Ingredients:

2 large or 4 small chicken breasts

2 parsnips - 2 carrots

1 acorn squash

1 x 14.5 oz can of chicken broth

garlic (pre-chopped) – as much as you like

salt

pepper

nutmeg

honey

Directions:

Peel and chop carrots and parsnips and place them in the bottom of the crock pot.

Sprinkle with garlic.

Place chicken on top.

Pour in broth.

Cut squash into chunks and slice off the skin.

Place on top of chicken.

Sprinkle desired amounts of salt, pepper and nutmeg on top of squash and drizzle enough honey on top to lightly cover the squash.

Cook on low 8-10 hours.

# BOURBON BREAST OF CHICKEN

Ingredients:

4 chicken breasts halves

¼ c. flour

½ tsp paprika

Salt

2 tbsp butter

2 tbsp oil

2 tbsp onion, chopped

2 tbsp parsley, chopped

¼ tsp dried chervil

¼ c. bourbon

1 (4 oz) can mushrooms, undrained

1 (10 oz) can tomatoes

¼ tsp sugar (or natural sugar alternative)

Salt & Pepper

Directions:

Dredge chicken in flour which has been mixed with paprika and a little salt.

Heat butter and oil in a skillet and saute chicken on both sides until lightly browned.

Stir in onion, parsley and chervil and cook a moment. Remove from heat.

Place chicken in crock cooker.

Combine remaining ingredients and pour over chicken.

Cover and cook on low for 6 to 7 hours.

Serve with noodles of rice.

Serves 4

## CREAM CHEESE CHICKEN CROCK

Ingredients:

4lbs of breast and rib chicken pieces cut up

2 tbsp melted butter

salt and pepper to taste

1 package of dry Italian seasoning mix

1 can cream of chicken soup

1 x 8 oz brick of cream cheese, cut up in cubes

½ c. chicken broth

1 large onion

crushed garlic to taste

Directions:

Brush chicken with butter and sprinkle with the dry Italian seasoning mix.

Cover and cook on low for 6-7 hours.

About 45 minutes before done, brown the onion in the butter and then add the cream cheese, soup, and chicken broth to the saucepan.

Add the crushed garlic and stir all ingredients until smooth. Add salt and pepper to taste.

Pour sauce mixture over chicken in crock pot and cook an additional 30-45 minutes.

Remove chicken to platter and stir sauce before pouring over.

## BRAISED CHICKEN CURRY WITH YAMS (sweet potatoes)

Ingredients:

Oil

2 lbs chicken legs and thighs chicken cut into chunks

2 large white onions chopped

1 tbsp minced garlic

1 tbsp minced ginger

1/3 cup madras curry powder (mild, medium/hot your choice)

1 banana

2 bay leaves

4 cups chicken stock

3 large yams, peeled and chopped

salt and black pepper to taste

Directions:

In a hot stock pot or large saucepan coated with oil, season the chicken and brown on all sides.

Put chicken aside.

In the same pot, remove all chicken fat, leaving only a coating of oil and saute onions, garlic and ginger.

Then add curry powder.

Mix quickly for 2 minutes making sure not to burn the curry powder.

Put into crock pot.

Put all chicken, broth, banana and all other ingredients now into the crock pot and leave on low for 4 hours.

Add seasonings.

Serve on basmati rice.

## BROWN RICE AND CHICKEN

Ingredients:

1 c. diced chicken

2 onions, chopped

2 stalks celery, chopped

2 c. cooked rice

¼ c. dry white wine

2 c. chicken broth

1 c. sliced almonds

Directions:

Combine all ingredients in slow cooker.

Cook on low 6 to 8 hours or on automatic 4 to 5 hours.

Serve with sliced almonds lightly toasted.

## CAFE CHICKEN

Ingredients:

4 lbs cut up chicken

1 onion chopped

2 (or more) cloves of garlic, chopped (not pressed)

1 green pepper chopped

1 medium ripe tomato, peeled & chopped (I omitted, didn't have)

1 cup dry white wine

Pinch of Cayenne pepper

Directions:

Combine all ingredients in slow-cooker.

Cover, set on low and cook for 6-8 hours.

If you want you can cook for 5 1/2 and then place chicken on cookie sheets with sides and cook for 30-45 minutes at 350°F to crisp up skin.

Serve with crusty french bread.

Serves 4-5.

## CARROT CHICKEN

Ingredients:

skinless, boneless chicken breasts

1 medium head cabbage, quartered

1 pound carrots, cut into 1" pieces

water to cover

4 cubes chicken bouillon

1 teaspoon poultry seasoning

¼ teaspoon Greek-style seasoning

2 tablespoons cornstarch

¼ cup water

Directions:

Rinse chicken and place in slow cooker.

Rinse cabbage and place on top of chicken, then add carrots.

Add enough water to almost cover all.

Add bouillon cubes and sprinkle liberally with poultry seasoning.

Add Greek seasoning to taste (as you would salt and pepper).

Cook on low for 8 hours OR on high for 4 hours.

To Make Gravy:

When you're nearly ready to eat, pour off some of the juice

and place in a saucepan. Bring to a boil. Dissolve cornstarch or another flour of choice in about ¼ cup water (depending on how thick you like your gravy).

Add to saucepan and simmer all together until thick.

If desired, season with additional Greek seasoning.

Serve gravy over chicken and potatoes, if desired.

# CHICKEN A LA KING

Ingredients:
1 can cream of chicken soup or make your own
3 tbsp. flour
¼ tsp. pepper
Dash of cayenne pepper
1 lb. boneless, skinless chicken breasts, cut into cubes
I celery rib, chopped
½ c. chopped green pepper
¼ c. chopped onion
1 package (10 oz) frozen peas, thawed
2 tbsp. diced pimentos, drained
Hot cooked rice

Directions:
Combine soup, flour and peppers in crock pot, stir until smooth.
Stir in chicken, celery, onion and green pepper.
Cover and cook on low 7-8 hours or until meat is cooked through.
Stir in peas and pimentos.
Cook 30 minutes longer.
Serve over rice.

## QUICK CHICKEN & NOODLES

Ingredients:

4 carrots, sliced

4-5 pieces chicken

1 small onion, chopped

2 cups water

4 chicken bouillon cubes

1 tsp garlic salt

salt & pepper, to taste

1 lb egg noodles

Directions:

Place carrots in crock pot followed by all ingredients except noodles.

Cook on low for 8 hours.

At the end of cooking time, cook egg noodles on stove top.

While noodles cook, remove chicken from crock pot & cut into bite-size pieces.

Return chicken & noodles to CP.

If desired, thicken broth with cornstarch & water.

Just be sure to add some of the broth to your cornstarch mixture first.

This will prevent any lumps from forming.

# CHICKEN AND TURKEY SAUSAGE PAELLA

Ingredients:

2 ½ to 3 lbs. meaty chicken pieces

1 tbsp. cooking oil

8 oz cooked smoked turkey sausage, halved lengthwise and sliced

1 large onion, sliced

3 cloves garlic, minced

2 tbsp. snipped fresh thyme or 2 tsp. dried thyme, crushed

¼ tsp. black pepper

1/8 tsp. thread saffron or 1/4 tsp. ground turmeric

1 can chicken broth (low salt one)

½ c. water

2 c. chopped tomatoes

2 yellow or green sweet peppers, cut into very thin bite-size strips

1 c. frozen green peas

3 c. hot cooked rice

Directions:

Skin chicken.

Rinse chicken; pat dry.

In a large skillet, brown chicken pieces, half at a time, in hot oil.

Drain off fat.

Place in crock pot chicken pieces, turkey sausage, and onion.

Sprinkle with garlic, dried thyme (if using), black pepper, and saffron or turmeric.

Pour broth and water over all.

Cover; cook on low-heat setting for 7 to 8 hours or on high-heat setting for 3 ½ to 4 hours.

Add the tomatoes, sweet peppers, peas, and if using, the fresh thyme to the cooker.

Cover; let stand for 5 minutes.

Serve over the hot rice.

## CHICKEN CACCIATORE

Ingredients:
1 large onion, thinly sliced
1 ½ lb. skinless, boneless chicken breasts
2 (6 oz each) cans tomato paste
8 oz fresh sliced mushrooms
½ tsp. salt
¼ tsp. pepper
2 cloves garlic, minced
1 tsp. oregano
½ tsp. basil
1 bay leaf
¼ c. dry white wine
¼ c. water

Directions:
Put sliced onion in bottom of crock pot.
Add chicken pieces.
Stir together tomato paste, mushrooms, salt, pepper, garlic, herbs, white wine and water.
Spread over chicken.
Cover; cook on Low 7 to 9 hours (High: 3 to 4 hours).
Serve chicken pieces over hot spaghetti or vermicelli.
Serves 4

## EXTRA RICH CHICKEN CACCIATORE

Ingredients:

1 chicken (5 pounds), cut into pieces

¼ cup olive oil

1 cup flour

1 cup chopped onions

1 cup sliced mushrooms

1 cup carrots sliced lengthwise

1 cup green pepper sliced lengthwise

2 Tablespoons minced garlic

8 cups chopped, peeled tomatoes

½ cup tomato paste

¾ cup red or Marsala wine

1 teaspoon oregano

1 teaspoon basil

1 ½ teaspoons salt

1 teaspoon pepper

freshly grated Romano cheese

Instructions:

Wash and drain the chicken pieces.

Heat the oil in a deep skillet.

Roll and coat each chicken piece in the flour and brown each piece on all sides to a golden brown.

Transfer the chicken to paper towels to drain.

Saute the onion, mushrooms, carrots, green peppers, and garlic in the same skillet for 10 minutes.

Add the tomatoes and saute for another 5 minutes.

Stir in the tomato paste, wine, herbs, salt and pepper, and cook over medium heat for another 5 minutes.

Add all the chicken pieces and mix well then put all ingredients into the crock pot and cook on low for about 5 hours.

Serve over noodles and add grated cheese.

## CHICKEN CORDON BLEU

Ingredients:

4-6 chicken breasts (pounded out thin)

4-6 slices of swiss cheese (or mozzarella)

Slices of ham (optional)

1 can cream of mushroom soup (can use any cream soup) or you can make your own with broth, milk and flour

¼ c. milk

Salt and pepper to suit taste

Directions:

Wrap cheese around chicken.  Wrap the ham around first if using.

Roll up and secure with a toothpick.

Place chicken in crock pot.

Layer the rest on top.

Mix soup and milk.

Pour over top of chicken.

Cover and cook on low for 4 hours or until chicken is no longer pink.

Serve over noodles.

## SIMPLE CHICKEN IN A POT

Ingredients:

3lb whole chicken

2 carrots, sliced

2 onions, sliced

2 celery stalks with leaves,

1 ts basil

2 ts salt

½ ts black pepper

½ c. chicken broth or wine

Directions:

Put carrots, onions, and celery in bottom of crock pot.

Add whole chicken.

Top with salt, pepper, liquid.

Sprinkle basil over top.

Cover and cook until done-low 8 to 10 hours. (High 3 to 4 hours, using 1 cup water extra).

Remove chicken and vegetables with spatula.

# CHICKEN NOODLE SOUP

Ingredients:

3 carrots, peeled and cut into chunks

3 stalks celery, cut into chunks

1 large onion, quartered

3 boneless skinless chicken breast halves

2 cans chicken broth- fat free

2 to 3 soup cans of water

a generous shake of dried dill and a generous shake of dried parsley

8 oz noodles

Directions:

Put vegetables in crock pot.

Add chicken.

Pour in broth and water.

Add dill and parsley.

Cover and cook on low 8 hours.

Remove veggies and chicken from crock pot.

Add noodles, turn to high and heat while you shred the chicken and mince the veggies. You can run the veggies through the food processor.

Return chicken and veggies to crock pot and heat through.

It takes the noodles about 20 minute to cook.

# TRADITIONAL CHICKEN STEW

Ingredients:

2 lb chicken breasts/skinless Boneless/ cut in 1" cubes

2 c. fat-free chicken broth

3 c. potatoes; peel, cube

1 c. onion; chop

1 c. celery; sliced

1 c. carrots; sliced thin

1 tsp paprika

½ tsp pepper

½ tsp rubbed sage

½ tsp dried thyme

6 oz no-salt-added tomato paste

¼ c. cold water

3 tbsp cornstarch

Directions:

In a slow cooker, combine the first 11 ingredients

Cover and cook on high for 4 hours

Mix water and cornstarch until smooth

Stir into stew.

Cook, covered, 30 minutes more or until the vegetables are tender.

## MEXICAN CHICKEN STEW

Ingredients:

2 lbs skinless boneless chicken breasts cut into 1 ½" pieces

4 med russet potatoes, peeled and cut very small

1 (15 oz) can mild salsa

1 (4 oz) can diced green chilies

1 (1 ¼ oz) pkg taco seasoning mix

1 (8oz) can tomato sauce

Directions:

Mix all ingredients together in crock pot, cook 7-9 hours on low.

Serve with warm flour tortillas.

You can also served corn with this.

## COQ AU VIN

Ingredients:

12 small white onions, peeled

4 lb roasting chicken, cut up

½ ts salt

¼ ts black pepper

¼ c. brandy or cognac

2 ea cloves garlic, peeled and crushed

¼ ts ground thyme

1 ea bay leaf

1 ½c. dry, strong red wine

5 tb flour

1 c. chicken bouillon

¾ lb fresh mushrooms, wiped and stemmed

1 tb butter or margarine

¼ ts salt

1 tb chopped fresh parsley

Directions:

Place the onions in the slow cooker.

Remove the fat from the vent of the chicken and dice it.

In a large skillet over medium heat, heat the fat until it is rendered.

Discard the shriveled bits and saute the chicken until well browned.

Season with ½ tsp salt and the pepper.

Warm the brandy in a ladle or a small saucepan.

Light it with match and pour it over the chicken.

When the flame dies, lift the chicken into the slow cooker and add the garlic, thyme, and bay leaf.

Pour the wine into the hot skillet and scrape up the pan juices.

Dissolve the flour in the bouillon, turn it into the skillet and bring to simmering, stirring briskly to prevent lumps.

Turn into the slow cooker.

Cover and cook on Low 7-9 hours.

Before serving: About 10 minutes before serving, in a medium skillet, saute the mushrooms in the butter over medium high heat.

In about 5 minutes, they will be tender and the moisture will have evaporated from the skillet.

Season with salt and add to the chicken casserole.

If the sauce seems thin, simmer it in the mushroom skillet long enough to thicken to the consistency of heavy cream.

Garnish the Coq au Vin with parsley before serving.

## BURGUNDY COQ AU VIN

Ingredients:
2- ½ lb chicken breasts
1 clove garlic crushed
1 teaspoon salt
¼ teaspoon pepper
½ teaspoon dried thyme
2/3 cups sliced green onions
1 cup chicken broth
8 small white onions, peeled
1 cup burgundy wine
½ lb whole mushrooms
chopped parsley
8 small new potatoes scrubbed

Directions:

In large skillet, saute green onions, remove and drain on paper towel.

Add chicken pieces to skillet and brown well on all sides. Remove the chicken when it has browned and set aside.

Put peeled onions, mushrooms, and garlic in crock pot. Add browned chicken pieces and green onions, salt, pepper, thyme, potatoes and chicken broth.

Cover and cook on Low 6 -8 hours (High 3-4). During the last hour add Burgundy and cook on high. Garnish.

## FIESTA CHICKEN

Ingredients:

2 tbsp oil

3 pounds boneless, skinless chicken breasts, cut into 1-inch pieces

1 med onion, chopped

1 tsp oregano

1 small jalapeno pepper, finely chopped

3 cloves garlic, minced

1 can (14 ½ ounce) Mexican style diced tomatoes

¼ tsp ground cumin

Directions:

Heat oil in skillet.

Cook chicken pieces until browned.

Remove and drain. Place onion, green bell pepper, garlic and jalapeno pepper in skillet and saute until slightly cooked.

Add all ingredients to crock pot and stir to combine.

Cover; cook on LOW 8 hours (HIGH 4 hours).

Serve on flour tortillas.

# GARLIC CHICKEN WITH CABBAGE

Ingredients:

1 whole chicken

½-to 1 whole red or white onion chopped

1 cabbage – red or white

2 tbsp butter or margarine

3-8 garlic cloves or use garlic salt/powder to you liking

salt and pepper to taste

Directions:

Season chicken and place in crock pot.

Add onion and garlic cloves and salt and pepper.

Fill slow cooker ¼-way with water, cover and cook on high 6-8 hours.

The chicken should fall off of the bone.

During the last hour of cooking the chicken, cut up 1 head of cabbage (remove core).

Place in a large pot of pan with a shallow amount of water – half to 1 cup.

Add two tablespoons of butter or margarine and sprinkle liberally with garlic salt and pepper.

Cover and cook on med-high heat for 20-30 minutes. Once chicken and cabbage are done, place some cabbage in a bowl and top with chicken and some of the chicken broth. Add seasonings as you like.

## GREEK CHICKEN

Ingredients:

6 skinless chicken breasts

1 lg. can tomato sauce

1 sm. can tomato puree

1 can sliced mushrooms

1 can ripe olives

1 tbsp. garlic

1 tbsp. lemon juice

1 tsp. oregano

1 onion, chopped

½ c. wine or brandy (optional)

2 c. rice

Salt to taste

Directions:

Wash and remove fat from chicken.

Bake in 350 degree oven for about an hour.

Meanwhile, combine all other ingredients except rice.

Put chicken and sauce in crock pot on low heat and cook for at least 4 hours to blend flavors.

Before serving, cook rice according to directions on box. Serve chicken and sauce over rice.

Serves 6.

## JERK CHICKEN

Ingredients:

(A traditional Jamaican dish adapted to the crock pot)

1 large onion, cut into 8 pieces

1 generous tablespoon chopped crystallized ginger

½ to 1 habanero pepper, seeded, deveined, and finely minced (wear

gloves!)

½ teaspoon ground allspice

2 tablespoons dry mustard

1 teaspoon freshly ground black pepper

2 tablespoons red wine or balsamic vinegar

2 tablespoons soy sauce

2 cloves garlic, crushed and minced

3 to 4 pounds chicken tenders

Ingredients:

Combine onion and ginger in a food processor

Process until finely chopped.

Add remaining ingredients, except chicken, and pulse until well combined.

Place chicken in a 3 ½ quart (or larger) crock pot and cover with sauce.  Cover, set on low, and cook for 6 to 8 hours. or until chicken is tender (3 to 4 hours on high).  4 servings.

## LAZY CROCK POT CHICKEN

Ingredients:
1 pkg. boneless chicken breasts
1 can cream of mushroom soup
¼ c. flour
1 jar sliced mushrooms
Salt, pepper and paprika

Directions:
Rinse chicken breasts.
Put salt, pepper and paprika on both sides.
Place in Crock Pot.
Mix other ingredients together.
Add to Crock Pot. Cook on low all day.
Serve over noodles, rice, or mashed potatoes.

# LEMON ROSEMARY CHICKEN

Ingredients:

½ c. lemon juice

1 tbsp. vegetable oil

1 garlic clove, crushed

1 teaspoon. dried rosemary

¼ teaspoon. salt

¼ teaspoon. pepper

1 ½ to 2 lbs boneless, skinless chicken breasts

Directions:

In a large food storage bag, place lemon juice, oil, garlic, rosemary, salt and pepper.

Add chicken.

Close bag and marinate in refrigerator 4 hours or overnight, turning bag frequently.

Place chicken in the crock pot and pour marinade over. Cover and cook for 6 to 8 hours, or until tender, basting occasionally with the marinade, if possible.

You may add frozen broccoli and carrots about 1 to 1 ½ hours before done.

Serves 4 to 6.

## LO-CAL CROCK POT CHICKEN

Ingredients:

2 med. onions, thinly sliced
2-3 lb. chicken, cut up and skinned
2 cloves garlic, minced
1 lg. can tomatoes
1 tsp. salt
¼ tsp. pepper
½ tsp. oregano, crushed
½ tsp. basil
½ tsp. celery seed
1 bay leaf

Directions:

Layer in order and cook on low 6-8 hours, or on high 2 ½ for 4 hours.

## LOW-FAT CHICKEN & VEGGIE BAKE

Ingredients:
8 boneless, skinless chicken breasts
2 cans whole potatoes, drained
1 tsp garlic powder
1 bottle fat free Italian salad dressing
1 pkg frozen veggies
1 can water chestnuts (optional)
salt & pepper

Directions:
Sprinkle chicken breasts with salt, pepper and garlic.
Put chicken in bottom of crock pot.
Add remaining ingredients.
Cook on high for 4-6 hours or on low for 8-10 hours.
Serves 8

## MEDITERRANEAN STYLE CHICKEN

Ingredients:
6 skinless and boneless chicken breasts
1 large can tomato sauce
1 small can tomato puree
1 can sliced mushrooms
1 can ripe olives, sliced or whole
1 tablespoon garlic
1 tablespoon lemon juice
1 teaspoon oregano
1 onion, chopped
½ cup wine or brandy (optional)
cooked rice
Salt to taste

Directions:
Wash and remove excess fat from chicken.
Combine all ingredients in the crock pot, except the rice.
Cover and cook on low for 6 to 8 hours.
Serve chicken and sauce over rice.
Serves 6.

# CREAMY CHICKEN AND BROCCOLI

Ingredients:

6 chicken breasts, boneless, skinless, cut in cubes and frozen

3 tbsp olive oil

1 (1.05 oz) pkg. dry Italian dressing mix

1 (11 oz) can cream of celery soup

1 (8 oz) pkg. cream cheese, cubed

¼ c chicken broth

1 lg. onion, chopped

½ lb fresh mushrooms, sliced

¼ tsp. garlic, minced

1 (10 oz) pkg. frozen broccoli florets

Directions:

Place the olive oil in a bowl.

Add the cubed chicken and cover completely.

Place the Italian dressing mix in a zip lock bag.

Add the chicken and shake to coat well.

Place the chicken in the crock pot.

Cover and cook on low 3 1/2 hours.

After 3 ½ hours while continuing to cook the chicken, oil a skillet and place over medium high heat and add the onion and mushrooms.

Add the cream cheese.

Stir in the soup and the chicken broth.

You can also add about ¼ c of the juice from the crock pot if you like.

Add the garlic and stir until the mixture becomes smooth.

You can also add some salt and pepper to taste.

Pour the mixture over the chicken.

Cover and continue to cook 1 hour.

A Quick Tip - The chicken cooks better and has less of tendency to dry out if frozen when placed in the crock pot. Cube the chicken before freezing to make it easier.

## ANGEL PASTA CHICKEN

Ingredients:

4 chicken breasts, boneless and skinless

½ c margarine

1 (1.05 oz.) pkg. Italian salad dressing mix

1 (11 oz) can golden mushroom soup

½ c white wine

1 (4 oz) pkg. onion and chive cream cheese

1 (8 oz) pkg. angel hair pasta or noodles

Directions:

In a small saucepan over low heat melt the margarine.

Add the soup and wine.

Stir in the salad dressing and cream cheese.

Continue to stir continuously until the cream cheese has completely melted and the mixture is smooth.

Pour the mixture over the chicken.

Cover and cook on low for 6 hours.

Cook the angel hair pasta according to package directions.

Serve the chicken over the pasta.

## LITTLE ITALY CHICKEN AND SPINACH LASAGNA

Ingredients:

2 (11 oz) cans cream of chicken soup

1 (10 oz) pkg. frozen spinach, thawed, drained

1 (9 oz) pkg. cooked chicken, diced

1 (8 oz) carton sour cream

1 c milk

½ c Parmesan cheese

1 small onion, chopped

½ tsp. salt

¼ tsp. pepper

1/8 tsp. nutmeg

9 lasagna noodles, uncooked

1 c mozzarella cheese, shredded

Directions:

Place the soup, spinach, chicken and sour cream in large mixing bowl.

Stir to combine.

Pour in the milk and continue stirring until mixed in well.

Add the onion and stir.

Sprinkle in the Parmesan cheese, salt, pepper and nutmeg.

Stir until well combined.

Place 3 lasagna noodles in the bottom of the crock pot.

Pour 1/3 of the spinach mixture over the top of the noodles.

Add 1/3 of the mozzarella cheese.

Continue with 2 more identical layers topping off with the mozzarella cheese.

Cover and cook on high 1 hour.

Reduce heat to low and continue cooking 5 hours.

If the noodles don't quite fit in the crock pot, you can break them down.

Serve with a side salad and toasted Italian bread.

## SWEET CRANBERRY CHICKEN

Ingredients:
6 chicken breasts, boneless and skinless
6 green onions, chopped
½ c dried cranberries
½ c dried apples, chopped
½ tsp. garlic, minced
2 tbsp brown sugar (try a natural sugar alternative)
2 tbsp water
1 tsp. lemon juice
2 tsp. butter or margarine

Directions:
Place the chicken in the bottom of a crock pot.
Sprinkle with the green onions.
Add the cranberries and apples.
Next add the garlic.
Sprinkle with the brown sugar.
Pour in the water and the lemon juice.
Dot the top with the butter.
Cover and cook on low for 6 hours.
The chicken can be seasoned with garlic salt and pepper before being placed in the crock pot. Just omit the minced garlic if you season.

## LEMON PUCKER CHICKEN

Ingredients:

4 chicken breasts, boneless and skinless

1 fresh lemon

1 tsp. lemon pepper

1 tsp. paprika

Directions:

Lay the chicken breasts in the bottom of the crock pot

Slice the lemon in half and squeeze the juice from 1/2 over the chicken.

Sprinkle with the lemon pepper and paprika.

Slice the remaining half of lemon into thin slices.

Lay the lemon slices on top of the chicken.

Cover and cook on high 4 hours.

1 tbsp of lemon juice can be used in place of squeezing the lemon. Garlic is also good in place of the paprika.

Orange juice and a fresh orange can be used for a little different taste

## OVERNIGHT SPICY ROASTED CHICKEN

Ingredients:

4 tsp. salt

2 tsp. paprika

1 tsp. cayenne pepper

1 tsp. onion powder

1 tsp, thyme

½ tsp. garlic powder

½ tsp. pepper

1 lg. roasting chicken

1 lg. onion, quartered

Directions:

Mix all the spices together in a large mixing bowl.

Wash the chicken well and pat dry. Discard any giblets.

Coat the chicken thoroughly with the spice mixture both inside and out.

Place the chicken in a pan and cover with saran wrap.

Refrigerate overnight. Remove the chicken from the refrigerator.

Place the onions in the cavity of chicken.

Place the chicken in the crock pot. Do not add any liquid. The chicken produces it's own juices as long as you don't remove the cover while cooking. Cover and cook on low 9 hours.

## SQUASH CHICKEN

Ingredients:

4 chicken breasts, boneless and skinless

2 carrots, peeled and chopped

2 parsnips, peeled and chopped

1 acorn squash, peeled and chopped

1 (14.5 oz) can chicken broth

½ tsp. garlic salt

¼ tsp. pepper

¼ tsp. nutmeg

¼ C honey

Directions:

Place the carrot and parsnips in the bottom of the crock pot.

Add the garlic salt being sure to cover all the vegetables.

Place the chicken pieces on top.

Add the broth.

Lay the squash on top of the chicken.

Sprinkle in the pepper and nutmeg.

Pour the honey over the top being sure to cover completely.

Cover and cook on low 8 hours.

## HONEY ME UP CHICKEN

Ingredients:

8 chicken thighs, boneless and skinless

½ tsp. ginger

½ tsp. salt

¼ tsp. pepper

1 c dried fruit, mixed of your choice

½ c honey

1/3 c chicken broth

1 medium onion, diced

Directions:

Lay the chicken thighs in the bottom of the crock pot.

Sprinkle in the ginger, salt and pepper being sure to cover the chicken well.

Add the dried fruit spreading it out evenly over the chicken.

Pour in the honey and chicken broth.

Sprinkle in the onion.

Cover and cook on low 8 hours.

# SPICY CHICKEN WINGS APPETISER

Ingredients:

4 lbs chicken wings

1 (12 oz) bottle chili sauce

3 tbsp lemon juice

¼ c molasses

2 tbsp Worcestershire sauce

4 dashes hot pepper sauce

1 tbsp hot salsa

2 tsp chili powder

1 tsp garlic powder

2 tsp salt

Directions:

In a large mixing bowl mix together the chili sauce, lemon juice, molasses, Worcestershire sauce, hot pepper sauce and salsa.

Sprinkle in the chili powder, garlic powder and salt.

Mix to combine well.

Place the wings in the crock pot.

Pour the sauce mixture over the top.

Cover and cook on low 4 hours.

Great for parties!

# Crock Pot Beans

# MIXED BEAN SOUP

Ingredients:

1 package 16 Bean Soup mix (throw away any packet of flavoring you get inside) or 16oz of any beans you like

3 bay leaves

1 tablespoon crushed oregano

Either: 2 cans no-fat chicken stock

Or: 2 cans of tomatoes plus water

Or: Fill the crock pot with water and freshly diced tomatoes.

Experiment with the stock you use according to taste.

Additional water to cover

3 stalks celery chopped (optional)

3 carrots diced

1 large onion chopped

3 cloves garlic sliced

Optional extras - handfuls of cabbage, chopped red potatoes and zucchini

Instructions:

Combine first 5 ingredients (liquid should cover mixture by 1"-2") in Crock Pot Cook on high for 2 hours.

Add remaining ingredients and shift cooker to low and cook for additional 3 hours.

For more zing, add cayenne or crushed red pepper when adding second set of ingredients.

Serve as complete meal or over rice or with chunks of healthy gluten-free bread.

Some people alternatively, soak the beans overnight with the bay leaves and then the cooking time is less the next day or they cook on very low overnight.

And some people put everything into the crock pot at once and leave to cook for 9 to 12 hours.

Choose any option to suit.

Freezes well.

## BARBECUED BEAN SOUP

Ingredients:

1 lb great northern beans, soaked

2 tsp salt

1 med onion, chopped

1/8 tsp ground pepper

6 cup water

¾ cup barbecue sauce

Directions:

Place all ingredients in crock pot except barbecue sauce.

Cover and cook on Low 10 to 16 hours.

Stir in barbecue sauce before serving.

## BLACK BEAN CHILI

Ingredients:

1 packet dry black beans

2 tbsp. oil

6 garlic cloves, minced or pressed

2 onions, chopped

1/4 tsp. crushed red pepper flakes (more if you like hot food)

1 tbsp. chili powder

1 tbsp. ground cumin

1 tsp. dried oregano

1 bay leaf

1 x 28 oz can chopped tomatoes in juice

2 c. water

6 oz can tomato paste

1 tbsp. red wine vinegar

2 cans contrasting beans (pinto, garbanzo, great northern, etc.)--drained and rinsed

Grated cheese, sour cream, chopped parsley, onion, etc.

Directions:

Rinse and sort the beans and place in the crock pot with a generous amount of water.

Cook on low overnight (no presorting necessary).

In the morning drain the cooking water.

Heat the oil in a skillet and saute the onions, garlic and red pepper flakes.

Cook 1 minute, then add chili powder and cumin and cook 2 minutes, stirring.

Add this mixture to the slow cooker along with all remaining ingredients except canned beans and garnishes.

Stir well and cook on low all day.

Stir in canned beans an hour or so before serving.

Serve with garnishes.

## BLACK BEAN SOUP

Ingredients:
2 onion, chopped
2 cloves garlic, minced
3 tablespoons butter
1 pound black beans, soaked overnight, drained
1 stalk celery, chopped
1 bay leaf
½ cup sherry, or dry white wine
salt and pepper, to taste

Directions:
Saute onions and garlic in butter until transparent.
Combine with beans, celery, bay leaf, and 2 quarts water in the crock pot.
Cook on high, for 2 hours, then on low for 8 to 10 hours.
Remove bay leaf.
Puree soup and return to pot.
Add sherry, salt and pepper and heat through. Serve in soup bowls garnished with chopped hard-boiled eggs, parsley, and lemon slices.

## WHITE BEAN SOUP

Ingredients:

1 lb small white beans

8 c. water

1 c. onion, diced

1 c. celery, chopped

2 tb parsley, chopped

1 ts salt

1/4 ts pepper

1 bay leaf

Directions:

Assemble ingredients in Slow Cooker.

Cover and cook on low 8-10 hours or until beans are tender.

## AZTEC BLACK BEANS

Ingredients:

1 lb. dried black beans (or turtle beans)

16 oz jar of salsa (your favorite kind)

Directions:

Rinse black beans, removing any stones or foreign objects.

Cover with water, soak all night.

Drain beans and place in crock pot with salsa.

Add enough water to just cover beans.

Cover and cook on low 8-10 hours.

## BAKED BEANS SUPREME

Ingredients

2 cans white kidney beans

2 cans black beans

2 cans red kidney beans

1 can chick peas

2 diced onions

2 tablespoons mustard (from the fridge - the wet kind)

1 c. molasses

½ c. brown sugar

¾ c. maple syrup

Directions:

Rinse and drain beans and set aside.

On bottom of crock pot place diced onions, then pour in all beans no need to mix.

Then drizzle on all other ingredients. If mustard stays lumpy - it's ok.

DON'T STIR. It will look dry for awhile. Heat on high for about 6 hours stirring once about ¾ of the way through.

Serve over toast or pasta etc.

## BLACK BEAN CHILI SOUP

Ingredients:
2 x 15 oz cans black beans, drained and rinsed
2 x 4.5 oz cans 4.5 oz, each, chopped green chiles
1 can 14.5 oz Mexican Stewed tomatoes, undrained
1 can 14.5 oz diced tomatoes, undrained
1 can 11 oz, whole kernel corn, drained (I used a 16 oz can)
4 green onions, sliced
2 to 3 tbsp. chili powder
1 tsp. ground cumin (optional)
½ tsp. dried minced garlic

Directions:
Combine all ingredients in a 3 or 5 qt. slow cooker.
Cover and cook on high 5 to 6 hours.
Makes 8 cups. You can cook it low all day.
Serve it with shredded cheddar and fat free sour cream.

## BLACK EYED PEAS

Ingredients:

1 x 16 oz bag of dried black-eyed peas

1 x 14 ½ oz can of diced tomatoes with jalapenos

1 x 14 ½ oz can of diced tomatoes with mild green chiles

2 x 10 ½ oz cans of chicken broth

1 stalk of celery, chopped

salt and pepper to taste (it doesn't need much, if any)

Directions:

Pre-soak black-eyed peas according to the instructions on the bag.

Combine all ingredients and cook on low for 8-10 hours.

Serve with rice etc.

# Crock Pot Beef

# ALL DAY CROCK POT BEEF

Ingredients:

2-3 lbs. boneless beef cubes

½ c. flour

¼ c. butter

1 onion, sliced

1 tsp. salt

1/8 tsp. pepper

1 clove garlic, minced

2 c. beer (preferably low sugar or natural)

1/4 c. flour

Directions:

Coat beef cubes with the ½ cup flour.

Brown in melted butter.

Drain off excess fat.

In crock pot, combine browned meat with onion, salt, pepper, garlic and beer.

Cover and cook on low 5-7 hours (all day) until meat is tender.

Turn control to high. Dissolve remaining 1/4 cup flour in small amount of water.

Stir into meat mixture, cook on high 30-40 minutes.

Serve with rice and salad.

## BARBEQUE BEEF STEW

Ingredients:

2 lbs. stew meat

3 tbsp. oil

* 1 c. onion, sliced

½ c. green pepper, chopped

1 lg. clove garlic

½ tsp. salt

1/8 tsp. pepper

2 c. beef stock

1 can (8 oz) tomatoes

1 can (4 oz) mushrooms

1/3 c. barbecue sauce

3 tbsp. cornstarch

¼ c. cold water

Directions:

Saute onion, pepper and garlic in oil.

Add salt, pepper, beef stock, tomatoes, mushrooms and barbecue sauce. Cook in crock pot on low heat 8-10 hours.

Mix cornstarch, cold water and thicken before serving.

Serve over hot cooked rice.

## BARBECUE STEAK

Ingredients:

1 ½ lb boneless chuck steak, 1 1/2" thick

1 clove garlic, peeled and minced

¼ cup wine vinegar

1 tbsp brown sugar (or natural alternative)

1 tsp paprika

2 tbsp Worcestershire sauce

½ cup organic sugar free tomato sauce

1 tsp salt

1 tsp dry or prepared mustard

¼ tsp black pepper

Directions:

Cut the beef on a diagonal, across the grain into slices 1" wide.

Place these in the crock pot. In a small bowl, combine the remaining ingredients.

Pour over the meat, and mix.

Cover and cook on Low for 3 to 5 hours.

## BEER MEATBALLS

Ingredients:

1 can of beer

1 x 6 oz can spicy V-8 juice

1 tsp. lemon juice

1 tsp. hot sauce

½ c. Italian bread crumbs

1 c. onions

Salt and pepper to taste

1 lg. bottle sugar free tomato sauce (organic)

1 tsp. horseradish

1 tsp. Worcestershire sauce

2 to 3 lbs. ground beef

2 to 3 eggs

Directions:

Combine ground beef, ½ cup onions, Italian bread crumbs, eggs.

Make the mixture into small meatballs.

Then fry or bake the meat. In saucepan combine remaining ingredients.

Simmer for 15 minutes.

Put meatballs and sauce into slow cooker.

The sauce should cover the meat. Allow to simmer for at least 3 hours, however, the longer you let them simmer, the better they are!

6 to 10 hours on low temperature is great.

Stir them occasionally.

You may wish to add more ketchup, or V-8 juice - spice them up if you like them hot.

## CHILI BEEF DINNER

Ingredients:
2 lbs. ground beef
1 lg. onion
1 lg. green pepper
1 lg. jalapeno pepper
Chili powder to taste
Garlic salt to taste
Salt to taste
Pepper to taste
Xylitol sugar or stevia to taste
2 cans crushed tomatoes
1 can tomato puree
1 can kidney beans
2 cans chili hot beans

Directions:
Brown beef.
Saute chopped onion and green pepper in grease.
Mix beef, onion and green pepper.
Add spices; let stand 1 hour.
Add tomatoes, tomato puree, beans; cook in crock pot all day.
Best if refrigerated and warmed the next day.

# LATE BREAKFAST BRUNCH CASSEROLE

Ingredients:

1 ½ lb ground beef

1 ea onion -- large; finely chopped

2 tbsp olive oil or butter

2 ea garlic -- cloves; minced

Mushrooms sliced

2 tsp Salt

½ tsp nutmeg

½ tsp oregano -- leaf

½ pk spinach -- chopped; thawed from frozen and drained

3 tbsp flour

6 ea eggs -- beaten

¼ c. milk -- scalded

½ c. cheddar cheese -- sharp; grated

Directions:

In a pan, lightly brown ground beef and onion in olive oil;

Saute the mushrooms as well.

Drain well.  Place in well-greased crock pot.

Stir in remaining ingredients except eggs, milk and cheese until well blended.

Beat eggs and milk together.

Pour over other ingredients; stir well.

Dust with additional nutmeg.

Cover and cook on low setting for 7 to 10 hours or until firm. Make sure eggs not runny unless they are organic!

Just before serving, sprinkle with grated cheese.

6 to 8 servings

## BEEF AND BEANS LUNCH

Ingredients:

1 ½ lbs of stewing beef

1 tbsp. prepared mustard

1 tbsp. taco seasoning

½ tsp. salt

¼ tsp. pepper

2 garlic cloves minced

1 can 16 oz diced tomatoes, undrained

1 med. onion chopped

1 can Kidney beans rinsed and drained

1 can chili beans

1 can of black beans

Directions:

Combine mustard, taco seasonings, salt , pepper and garlic in a large bowl.

Add beef and toss to coat!

Put the beef in your crock pot and add the rest of the ingredients.

Cover and cook for 6 -8 hours on LOW.

Serve over hot rice!

## WINTER 4 BEAN CHILI

Ingredients:

1-2 pounds browned ground beef

2 cans chili hot beans

2 cans dark red kidney beans, drained

2 cans pinto beans, drained

2 cans kidney beans, drained

2 cans rotel tomatoes

1 package chili seasoning

Directions:

Put all ingredients in crock pot and cook on low all day (about 10 hours).

Serve with rice, couscous, pasta, quinoa or bread.

## BLACK BEAN CHILI

Ingredients:

¾ cup cooked black beans

1 lb. stew beef, cubed

3 tbsp oil

¼ cup chopped onion

¼ cup chopped green peppers

½ cup diced green chilies

3 tbsp. tomato paste

3 to 4 beef bouillon cubes, or beef base

¼ tsp. ground cumin

1 tsp. minced garlic

½ tsp. salt and pepper

1 cup shredded Monterrey Jack OR cheddar cheese

Directions:

Brown stew beef in oil with onion and green pepper.

Combine all ingredients except cheese and cook 6 to 8 hours on low.

Sprinkle cheese over individual servings.

## BEEF BOURGUIGNON

Ingredients:
1 cup dry red wine
2 tbsp olive oil
1 large onion -- sliced
½ tsp thyme
2 tbsp parsley -- chopped
1 bay leaf
¼ teaspoon pepper
2 pounds stewing beef, cut into 1½-inch cubes
12 small white onions
½ pound sliced mushrooms
2 cloves garlic -- minced
1 tsp salt

Directions:
Combine first seven ingredients, mix well, add beef.
Marinate at least 3 hours (overnight if refrigerated).
Drain meat, reserving marinade.
Brown meat in a pan.
Combine beef, vegetables and seasonings in slow cooker.
Pour over enough marinade to cover.
Cook on low 8-10 hours.

## BEEF BURGER STROGANOFF

Ingredients:
1 ½ lbs lean ground beef
1 small onion, chopped
2 tbs flour
¼ tsp paprika
1 tsp salt
1 can (10 3/4oz) condensed cream of mushroom soup
2 tbsp dry red wine
1 cup dairy sour cream
6 to 8 hamburger buns, toasted and buttered

Directions:
In large skillet, brown beef until red color disappears.
Drain.
In crock pot, mix together drained beef, onion, flour, paprika, and salt.
Stir in undiluted soup and wine.
Cover pot and cook on low 4 to 5 hours.
Stir in sour cream. Spoon mixture over toasted buns. Serves 6 to 8.
Serve over buttered noodles instead for a rich sensation!

## BEEF BURGUNDY

Ingredients:

2 pounds sirloin tip or round steak -- cut in 1 inch cubes

¼ cup flour

1 teaspoon salt

½ teaspoon seasoned salt

¼ teaspoon marjoram

¼ teaspoon thyme

¼ teaspoon pepper

1 clove garlic -- minced

1 cube beef bouillon -- crushed

1 cup Burgundy wine

2 tablespoons cornstarch (dissolved in water)

Fresh mushrooms (optional)

Directions:

Coat beef with flour and brown on all sides in a pan greased with butter.

Combine steak, seasonings, bouillon and Burgundy in crock pot.

Cover and cook on low for 6 to 8 hours or until meat is tender.

Turn control to high. Add cornstarch (cook on high 15 minutes) and mushrooms if you wish. Serves 6

**BEEF FAJITAS**

Ingredients:

1 ½ pounds beef flank steak

1 cup chopped onion

1 green sweet pepper, cut into ½ inch pieces

1 jalapeno pepper, chopped

1 tbsp. cilantro

2 garlic cloves, minced (or ¼ tsp. garlic powder)

1 tsp. chili powder

1 tsp. ground cumin

1 tsp. ground coriander

½ tsp. salt

1 can (8oz) chopped tomatoes

12 x 8inch flour tortillas

Directions:

Toppings: sour cream, guacamole, shredded cheddar cheese and salsa

Cut flank steak into 6 portions.

In any size crock pot combine meat, onion, green pepper, jalapeno pepper, cilantro, garlic, chili powder, cumin, coriander and salt.

Add tomatoes.

Cover and cook on low 8-10 hours or high 4-5 hours.

Remove meat from crock pot and shred.

Return meat to crock pot and stir.

To serve, spread meat mixture into flour tortillas and top with toppings.

Roll up.

# BEEF N BREW VEGETABLE SOUP

Ingredients:

3 medium onions, sliced

1 lb carrots, cut into ½" slices

4 parsnips, cut into ½" slices

2 bay leaves

4 cloves garlic, minced

1 tbsp snipped fresh thyme or 1 tsp dried thyme, crushed

½ tsp pepper

2 tbsp quick cooking tapioca

1 ½ lbs beef stew meat, cut into 1" cubes

1 x 14 ½ oz can beef broth

1 x 12 oz can beer

Directions:

In a 5 or 6 quart crock pot, place onions, carrots, parsnips, garlic, bay leaves, dried thyme, and pepper.

Sprinkle with tapioca.

Place meat on top of vegetables.

Add beef broth and beer.

Cover; cook on low-heat setting for 10 to 12 hours or on high-heat setting for 5 to 6 hours.

To serve, remove bay leaves; if using fresh thyme, stir in now.

## BEEF POT ROAST

Ingredients:

1 ½ lb- 2lb. pot roast meat

1 dry package of Garlic Dressing

1 dry pkg of Italian (or Zesty Italian) Dressing

1 can of beer (your choice-not dark)

Directions:

Place garlic dressing in bottom of crock pot.

Place meat on top, top with other dressing and pour beer over all. Let cook 8-10 hours on low.

Serve with potatoes.

# BEEF STEW

Ingredients:

1 lb. beef bourguignon (or cheaper cut)

3 large sweet potatoes (cut into 1" thick slices)

2 cans beef bouillon (or broth or consommée)

2 small cans organic tomato paste

3-4 handfuls of assorted veggies (can use frozen green & yellow beans and carrots)

1 lb. fresh mushrooms (quartered)

1 large onion (diced)

2 cloves garlic (minced)

¼ cup flour

Directions:

Mix bite sized pieces of meat in flour, brown in some oil along with the diced garlic.

While meat is browning, combine beef bouillon & tomato paste in a crock pot, mix well.

Pre-cook the sweet potatoes until just tender, add to crock pot along with onions and any raw veggies that you may use.

Add enough water to cover and cook on low for as long as you want probably about 5 hours is enough. You can add the frozen veggies and some quartered mushrooms for about the last 1 hour or so. Thicken with flour and water in the last hour if you wish.

## QUICK BEEF STEW

Ingredients:

1 package stew beef

1 can cream of potato soup

1 can cream of mushroom soup

1 - 1 ½ cans of water

Directions:

Cook on high all day (7-8) hours

Serve over wild rice.

## BEEF STROGANOFF

Ingredients:

2 lbs top round steak, sliced thin across the grain

1 lb fresh mushrooms, sliced

1 medium onion, sliced

¼ tsp thyme

¾ cup dry sherry or dry white wine (experiment with amounts)

¾ cup beef broth

¾ tsp dry mustard or tomato paste (choose either for different tastes

¼ tsp garlic salt

Directions:

Put all this in the crock pot, stir well and cook on low for 8 hours.

Turn heat to high and mix 1- ½ cup sour cream ½ cup flour, heat on high for 40 minutes.

Serve over rice or noodles.

## QUICK BEEF STROGANOFF

Ingredients:
1 can cream of mushroom soup
1 package onion soup mix
1 package mushroom
1 onion cut in rings
1 package beef stew meat
salt
pepper

Directions:
Put in crock pot and cook all day.
Add 16 oz sour cream before serving.
Serve over Egg Noodles.

## BEEF TACO BEAN SOUP

Ingredients:

2 lbs. rump roast

1 pk taco seasoning

1 can Mexican style diced tomatoes (15 oz)

1 small can green chiles

1 can tomato sauce (8 oz)

1 onion - chopped

2 beef bouillon cubes

2 cans red kidney beans, (15 oz each), rinsed, drained

Shredded cheddar cheese

Directions:

Cut roast into bite sized chunks.

Roll in taco seasoning and add to crock pot.

Then add the tomatoes, chiles, tomato sauce, onion, and bouillon cubes.

Cover and cook on low 6 hours or until meat is tender.

Add the drained beans and cook until the beans are heated through; around 30 minutes.

Serve topped with cheese, and the toppings that you like.

## BLACK BEAN & BEEF CHILI

Ingredients:

¾ cup cooked black beans

1 lb. stew beef, cubed

3 tablespoons oil

¼ cup chopped onion

¼ cup chopped green peppers

½ cup diced green chilies

3 tbsp. tomato paste

3 to 4 beef bouillon cubes, or beef base

¼ tsp. ground cumin

1 tsp. minced garlic

½ tsp. salt and pepper

1 cup shredded Monterrey Jack OR cheddar cheese

Directions:

Brown stew beef in oil with onion and green pepper.

Combine all ingredients except cheese and cook 6 to 8 hours on low.

Sprinkle cheese over individual servings.

## CABBAGE AND BEEF CASSEROLE

Ingredients:
2 lb. ground beef
1 head cabbage, shredded
1 small onion, chopped
1 (16oz) can tomatoes
broth or tomato juice to cover bottom of pot
Garlic salt, thyme, red pepper and a bit of oregano

Directions:
Brown ground beef and drain.
Shred cabbage and chop onion.
Put in broth or other liquid to cover bottom of pot.
Layer cabbage, onion, spices, meat, and garlic salt.
Repeat layers ending with beef.
Top with tomatoes, undrained and a dusting of oregano.
Cook on high for 1 hour. Stir all together.
Cook on low heat until ready to eat, 8-10 hours.
Makes 3-4 servings.

## CARNE GISADA

Ingredients:

3 lbs beef stew meat

2 cans diced tomatoes with green chilies or make your own from fresh

salt and pepper to taste

3 cloves garlic minced

1 cup chopped onion

3 tbsp flour

½ tsp cumin

½ tsp oregano

1 tsp chili powder

¼ cup water

1 diced bell pepper

Directions:

Place stew meat, ¼ cup water, salt and pepper in crock pot.

Turn heat to high and let simmer for 1 ½ hours. Drain juice from tomatoes into measuring cup.

Add tomatoes garlic and onions to crock pot STIR let simmer on high for 30 minutes.

Add cumin, oregano, and chili powder and stir.

Blend juice and enough water to equal 1½ cups liquid and flour stir into mixture. Let cook on LOW for 3-4 hours until sauce is nice and thick. Serve with warm flour tortillas.

# HAMBURGER CHILI

Ingredients:

2 onions, chopped

2 cloves garlic (I use the minced kind that comes in a jar)

1 lb. lean hamburger

2 tbsp chili powder

cumin to taste (I leave this out)

2 cans (16 oz ea.) tomatoes

2 cans tomato soup

2 cans kidney beans, drained

salt and pepper to taste

optional: shredded cheese or sour cream for topping

Directions:

Cook onions and garlic in 2 tbsp oil till onions are yellow.

Add hamburger and cook till browned.

Stir in chili powder and optional cumin; cook 2 minutes more.

Meanwhile, in crock pot, combine remaining ingredients.

Stir in browned meat mixture.

Cover and cook on Low setting for 8-10 hours.

To serve: ladle chili into bowls. Top with optional shredded cheese or sour cream, if desired.

## QUICK CHILI

Ingredients:

1 lb ground beef, cooked and rinsed

60-70 ounces rinsed light or dark kidney beans

16 ounces tomato paste

16 ounces peeled chopped tomatoes (reserve liquid)

½ small onion, chopped

1 small green pepper, chopped

1 package chili seasonings

cayenne pepper to taste, if desired

Directions:

Put all ingredients in the crock pot and cook on low until you are ready, I'd recommend at least 5 hours so the peppers and onions are cooked soft.

Use the reserved tomato liquid if it seems too thick for your taste.

We serve with tortillas, cheese, sour cream, and salsa!

## CHILI CON CARNE

Ingredients:

4 pounds ground beef

3 tablespoons shortening

2 cups chopped onion

2 garlic cloves -- crushed

4 tablespoons chili powder

3 beef bouillon cubes -- crushed

1 ½ teaspoons paprika

1 teaspoon oregano

1 teaspoon ground cumin

½ teaspoon cayenne pepper

½ cup beef stock

1 can tomatoes - 28 oz.

1 can tomato paste - 8 oz

4 cans red kidney beans - 1 lb cans

Directions:

Heat shortening in skillet and brown beef, discard fat.

Combine all ingredients in removable liner, stirring well.

Place liner in base.

Cover and cook on low 8-10 hours; high 4-5 hours or auto 6-7 hours.

## GREEK STEW

Ingredients:

3 pounds of stewing beef

1 ½ pounds small onions (about 7)

3 cloves garlic, minced

1- 28 oz can tomatoes

½ cup beef stock

1- 5 ½ oz can tomato paste

2 tbsp red wine vinegar

2 tsp dried oregano & ½ tsp each salt & pepper

½ cup all purpose flour

½ cup cold water

1 sweet green pepper, chopped

Decoration: ½ c. feta cheese, 2 tbsp. chopped fresh parsley

Directions:

Cut beef into 1 inch cubes, trimming off any fat.

Cut onions into wedges. Put meat & onions into slow cooker along with garlic & tomatoes.

Combine beef stock, vinegar, oregano, salt & pepper and add to slow cooker, stirring gently to blend.

Cook on Low for 8-9 hours or High for 6 hours. Add flour & water mixture and chopped green pepper. Cook on high for 15 minutes or until thickened. Serve sprinkled with feta & parsley.

# MEXICAN CHILI

Ingredients:

2 (15½ oz) cans red kidney beans, drained

1 (28 oz) can tomatoes, cut up

1 c. chopped celery

1 c. chopped onion

1 (6 oz) can tomato paste

½ c. chopped green pepper

1 (4 oz) can green chili peppers, drained and chopped

2 tbsp. sugar

1 bay leaf

½ tsp. garlic powder

1 tsp. salt

1 tsp. dried, crushed marjoram

Dash of pepper

1 lb. ground beef

Directions:

In skillet brown ground beef and drain.

In crock pot combine all ingredients.

Cover, cook on low heat for 8 to 10 hours. Remove bay leaf and stir before serving.

Approximately 10 servings

# Crock Pot Vegetables

# ASPARAGUS CASSEROLE

Ingredients:

2 cans sliced asparagus, (10 oz each)

1 can cream of celery soup, (10 oz)

2 hard cooked eggs, thinly sliced

1 cup grated cheddar cheese

½ cup coarsely crushed saltines or Ritz crackers

1 teaspoon butter

Directions:

Place drained asparagus in lightly buttered crock pot.

Combine soup and cheese.

Top asparagus with sliced eggs, soup mixture, then the cracker crumbs. Dot with butter.

Cover and cook on low for 4 to 6 hours.

## BROCCOLI & CHEESE SOUP

Ingredients:
2 c. cooked noodles
1 (10 oz) pkg. frozen chopped broccoli, thawed
3 tbsp. chopped onions
2 tbsp. butter
1 tbsp. flour
2 cups shredded American cheese
Salt to taste
5 ½ c. milk

Directions:
Combine all ingredients in slow cooker.
Stir well.
Cook on low for 4 hours.
Makes 8 servings.

# CREAMY SCALLOPED POTATOES

Ingredients:

7 to 9 medium potatoes, thinly sliced

1 cup cold water

½ tsp cream of tartar

3 tbsp butter

1 medium onion, thinly sliced

¼ cup all-purpose flour

1 teaspoon salt & ¼ teaspoon ground black pepper

1 can (10 x ¾ ounces) condensed cream of mushroom soup

4 oz American cheese, slices or shredded

Directions:

Toss potato slices in 1 cup water and ½ teaspoon cream of tartar, then drain.

Put half of sliced potatoes in a buttered or greased 3 ½ to 4-quart slow cooker.

Top with half of onion slices, half of the flour, half of the salt and half of the pepper. Dot with half of the butter.

Repeat layers; dot with remaining butter. Spoon soup over the top.

Cover and cook on low 7 to 9 hours, or high 3 to 4 hrs. Add cheese about 30 minutes before serving.

Double ingredients for a 5-6-quart crock pot.

## CROCK POT ARTICHOKES

Ingredients:

5 artichokes, remove stalks and tough leaves

1 ½ ts salt

8 peppercorns

2 stalks celery, cut up

½ lemon, sliced

2 c. boiling water

Directions:

Combine all ingredients in crock pot.

Cook on high 4 - 5 hours.

# CROCK POT CAPONATA

Ingredients:

1 lb plum tomatoes chopped

1 eggplant in 1/2" pieces

2 med zucchini in 1/2" pieces

1 onion finely chopped

3 stalks celery sliced

½ c. chopped parsley

2 tbsp red wine vinegar

1 tbsp brown sugar (or natural alternatives)

¼ c. raisins

¼ c. tomato paste

1 tsp salt

¼ tsp freshly ground black pepper

3 tbsp oil cured black olives (optional)

2 tbsp capers (optional)

Directions:

Combine tomatoes, eggplant, zucchini, celery, onion, parsley, vinegar, sugar, raisins, tomato paste, salt & pepper in crock pot.

Cook, covered on low heat for 5 ½ hours. Do not remove cover during cooking. Stir in olives & capers, if using.

Serve warm or cold.

## GREEN BEAN & POTATO CASSEROLE

Ingredients:

About 6 cups fresh trimmed and cut green beans (about 2 pounds) or 2 x 16-ounce packages frozen cut green beans

4 to 6 medium red-skinned potatoes, sliced about 1/4-inch

1 large onion, sliced

1 tsp dried dill weed

1 tsp salt

½ teaspoon pepper

1 can cream of chicken soup or other cream soup, undiluted, or use about 1 cup of homemade seasoned white sauce, velouté or cheese sauce

margarine

Directions:

Lightly grease crock pot with butter.

Layer sliced potatoes, sliced onion and green beans, sprinkling with dill and salt and pepper as you go.

Dot with margarine, about 1 tablespoon total, and add about 2 tablespoons of water.

Cover and cook on high for 4 hours (low, about 8 hours).

Stir in soup or sauce; turn to low and cook an additional 30 minutes or leave on warm until serving time or up to 4 hours.

Serves 6 to 8.

# BAVARIAN RED CABBAGE

Ingredients:
1 large head of red cabbage, washed and coarsely sliced
2 med onions coarsely chopped
6 tart apples, cored & quartered
2 tsp. salt
2 c. hot water
3 tbsp sugar (natural alternative xylitol or stevia)
2/3 cup cider vinegar
6 tbsp butter

Directions:
Place all ingredients in the crock pot in order listed.
Cover and cook on low 8 to 10 hours (High: 3 hours).
Stir well before serving.

## CHEESE & POTATO CASSEROLE

Ingredients:

2 lb. pkg. frozen hash brown potatoes (partially thawed)

2 x 10 oz cans cheddar cheese soup

1 x 13 oz can evaporated milk

1 can French fried onion rings, divided

Salt and pepper to taste

Directions:

Combine potatoes, soup, milk, and half the can of onion rings;

Pour into greased slow cooker and add salt and pepper.

Cover and cook on low for 8 to 9 hours or high for 4 hours.

Sprinkle the rest of the onion rings of top before serving.

## CHEESE & ARTICHOKE DIP

Ingredients:

8 ounces process American cheese (Velveeta)

1 can (10oz) 98% fat-free cream of mushroom soup

2 tsp Worcestershire sauce

¼ cup evaporated milk

1 teaspoon dry mustard

1½ c. shredded cheddar cheese

1/3 c. chopped roasted red pepper

1 can artichoke hearts, drained and coarsely chopped

Directions:

Combine all ingredients in the crock pot.

Cover and cook on low for 2 to 3 hours, until melted.

Stir well and serve with assorted crackers, bread cubes, or chips.

You can also use this dip with cooked pasta for a delicious macaroni and cheese!

# CHEESY CAULIFLOWER & BROCCOLI

Ingredients:

1 (10 oz) pkg frozen cauliflower, thawed

1 (10 oz) pkg frozen broccoli, thawed

1 can Cheddar cheese soup

salt and pepper to taste

¼ cup shredded cheddar cheese, if desired

Directions:

Place broccoli and cauliflower in crockery pot.

Top with soup.

Season with salt and pepper.

Cover and cook on low for 4 to 5 hours.

About 20 minutes before done, top with cheddar cheese if used.

Serves 6 to 8.

## BROCCOLI SOUP

Ingredients:

4 c. water

4 chicken bouillon cubes or veg cubes

¼ c. chopped onion

2 c. diced potatoes

1 bag frozen, chopped broccoli

2 cans cream of chicken soup

½ -1 lb. Velveeta cheese, cubed

Directions:

Mix water, bouillon cubes, onions, potatoes and broccoli in a crock pot.

Cook on high until broccoli is thawed.

Add cream of chicken soup and cheese, to taste, to mixture.

Turn crock pot on low and cook for 2 hours.

## CORN CHOWDER

Ingredients:

2 cans (16 oz) whole kernel corn, drained

2 to 3 medium potatoes, chopped

1 onion, chopped

½ teaspoon salt

pepper to taste

2 cups chicken broth

2 cups milk

¼ cup butter or margarine

Directions:

Combine first 6 ingredients in crock pot.

Cover and cook on low for 7 to 9 hours.

Puree in a blender or food processor, if desired, then return to pot.

Stir in milk and butter; cook on high about 1 hour more.

Serves 6 to 8.

# CREAMY SPINACH NOODLE CASSEROLE

Ingredients:

8 oz dry spinach noodles

2 tbsp. oil

1 ½ cups sour cream

1/3 cup all-purpose flour

1 ½ cups cottage cheese

4 green onions, minced

2 tsp. Worcestershire sauce

1 dash hot pepper sauce

2 tsp. garlic salt

Directions:

Cook noodles in a pot of salted, boiling water until just tender.

Drain and rinse with cold water. Toss with oil.

Combine sour cream and flour in a large bowl, mixing well.

Stir in cottage cheese, green onions, Worcestershire sauce, hot pepper sauce and garlic salt.

Fold noodles into mixture until well combined.

Generously grease the inside of a slow cooker and pour in noodle mixture.

Cover and cook on high for 1 ½ to 2 hours.

Makes about 5 servings.

## POTATO SOUP

Ingredients:

6-8 potatoes, chunked

2 med. carrots, cubed

2 stalks celery, cubed

1 med. onion, chopped

1 tbsp. parsley flakes

5 c. water

Salt and pepper to taste

Cook in crock pot on low for 8 hours or until vegetables are done. One hour before serving, add one can of evaporated milk.

## SPAGHETTI SQUASH

Ingredients:

2 c water

1 spaghetti squash, a size which will fit in a crock pot

Directions:

With a skewer or large fork, puncture several holes in the squash.

Pour water in the slow cooker, add the whole squash.

Cover and cook on low for 8 to 9 hours.

Split and remove seeds, then transfer the "spaghetti" strands to a bowl.

Serve tossed with butter and salt and pepper, Parmesan cheese or your favorite sauce.

## VEGETABLE CASSEROLE

Ingredients:

2 cups carrots, cut in strips, cooked & drained

2 cups celery, diced

1 onion, diced

¼ cup green pepper, diced

1 pint tomato juice

4 cups green beans, drained

1 teaspoon salt

dash of pepper

3 tbsp tapioca

1 tbsp xylitol or some stevia if desired

Directions:

Mix all ingredients together in slow cooker/Crock Pot.

Dot with 2 tablespoons margarine and cook on low for 8-10 hour or on high for 4-5 hours.

**VEGETABLE CURRY**

Ingredients:

4 medium carrots, bias sliced into inch slices

2 medium potatoes, cut into 1/2 cubes

5 oz can garbanzo beans, drained

8 oz green beans, cut into 1 pieces

1 cup coarsely chopped onion

3 to 4 cloves Garlic, minced

2 tbsp quick-cooking tapioca

2 tsp curry powder

1 tsp ground coriander

½ tsp crushed red pepper (optional)

¼ tsp salt

1/8 teaspoon Ground cinnamon

14 oz Can vegetable broth

16 oz Can tomatoes, cut up

2 cups Hot cooked rice

Directions:

In a 3½ 4, or 5 quart crockery cooker combine carrots, garbanzo beans, potatoes, green beans, onion, garlic, tapioca, curry powder, coriander, red pepper (if desired), salt, and cinnamon.

Pour broth over all.

Cover; cook on low-heat setting for 8 to 10 hours or on high-heat setting for 4 to 5 hours.

Stir in undrained tomatoes.

Cover; let stand 5 minutes.

Serve with cooked rice.

Makes 4 servings.

**VEGETABLE PASTA**

Ingredients:

2 tbsp butter or marg

1 zucchini, 1/4" slice

1 yellow squash, 1/4" slice

2 carrots, thinly sliced

1½ cups mushrooms, fresh, sliced

1 package broccoli, frozen, cuts

4 green onions, sliced

2 to 3 cloves garlic, minced

½ teaspoon basil, dried

¼ tsp salt

½ tsp pepper

1 cup parmesan cheese, grated

12 oz Fettuccine

1 cup mozzarella cheese shredded

1 cup cream

2 egg yolks

Directions:

Rub crock wall with butter.

Put zucchini, yellow squash, carrots, mushrooms, broccoli, onions, garlic, seasonings and parmesan in the Crock Pot.

Cover; cook on High 2 hours.

Cook fettuccine according to package directions; drain.

Add cooked fettuccine, mozzarella, cream and egg yolks.

Stir to blend well.

Allow to heat for 15 to 30 minutes.

For serving turn to Low for up to 30 minutes.

Serves 6.

## VEGETABLES ITALIAN-STYLE

Ingredients:

1 tsp salt

1 med eggplant, cut in 1" cubes

2 to 3 medium zucchini, halved & sliced ½"

1 large onion, sliced thinly

12 oz fresh mushrooms, sliced

1 tbsp olive oil

4 plum tomatoes, sliced ¼" thick

1½ cups mozzarella cheese, shredded

2 cups tomato sauce

1 tsp oregano

salt and pepper, to taste

Directions:

Toss eggplant and zucchini with the 1 teaspoon of salt.

Place in a large colander over a bowl to drain for about 1 hour.

Drain and squeeze excess moisture out.

In a large skillet over medium heat, saute onion, eggplant, zucchini, and mushrooms until slightly tender.

In the crock pot, layer 1/3 of the vegetables (including sliced tomatoes), 1/3 of the the tomato sauce. and 1/3 of the cheese.

Sprinkle with oregano, salt and pepper.

Repeat layering 2 more times.

Cover and cook on low 6 to 8 hours.

Serve over rice, pasta, or other grain.

Serves 6.

## ZUCCHINI CASSEROLE

Ingredients:

1 red onion, sliced

1 green pepper, cut in thin strips

4 med. zucchini, sliced & unpeeled

1 (16 oz) can diced tomatoes, undrained

1 tsp. salt

½ tsp. pepper

½ tsp. basil

1 tbsp. butter

¼ c. grated parmesan cheese

Directions:

Combine all ingredients, except oil and cheese, in a slow cooker.

Set temperature on low and heat for 3 hours.

Dot casserole with oleo and sprinkle with cheese.

Cook 1½ hours more on low setting.

Makes 6 servings.

# Crock Pot Miscellaneous

## BARLEY WITH MUSHROOMS & GREEN ONIONS

Ingredients:

1 cup barley

1 can (14 ½ oz) roasted garlic chicken broth (about 2 cups)

3 green onions, thinly sliced (about ½ cup)

4 to 6 ounces fresh or canned mushrooms, sliced

salt or seasoned salt and pepper to taste

2 teaspoons butter or margarine

Directions:

Combine all ingredients in crock pot.

Cover and cook on low for 4 to 4 ½ hours.

## CLASSIC SWISS FONDUE

Ingredients:
1 clove garlic
2 ½ cups dry white Rhine, Chablis or Riesling wine
1 tbsp lemon juice
1 lb. Swiss cheese, grated
½ lb. Cheddar cheese, grated
3 tbsp flour
3 tbsp kirsch
freshly ground nutmeg
pepper
paprika
1 loaf Italian or French bread, cut into 1-inch cubes

Directions:
Rub an enameled or stainless steel pan with garlic clove.
Heat wine to a slow simmer (just under boiling).
Add lemon juice.
Combine cheeses and flour and gradually stir in.
Using a figure-8 motion, stir constantly until cheese is melted.
Pour into lightly greased crock pot.

Add kirsch;

Stir well.

Sprinkle with nutmeg, pepper and paprika.

Cover and cook on high setting for 30 minutes, then turn to low setting for 2 to 5 hours.

Keep on Low setting while serving.

Using fondue forks, dip bread cubes into fondue.

## ALL DAY MACARONI CHEESE

Ingredients:

8 oz elbow macaroni, cooked and drained

4 c. (16 ounces) shredded sharp Cheddar Cheese

1 can (12 ounces) evaporated milk

1 ½ cups milk

2 eggs

1 teaspoon salt

½ teaspoon black pepper

Directions:

Place the cooked macaroni in greased crock pot.

Add the remaining ingredients, all except 1 cup of the cheese and mix well.

Sprinkle with the remaining 1 cup of cheese and then cover and cook on low setting for 5 to 6 hours or until the mixture is firm and golden around the edges.

Do not remove the cover or stir until it has finished cooking.

## NO EGGS MACARONI CHEESE

Ingredients:

1 (16 oz) pkg. macaroni, cooked & drained

1 tbsp. salad oil

1 (13 oz) can evaporated milk

1 ½ c. milk

1 tsp. salt

3 c. shredded sharp cheddar cheese

½ c. melted butter

Directions:

Lightly grease Crock Pot.

Toss macaroni and oil.

Add all remaining ingredients.

Stir, cover and cook on low 3 to 4 hours, stirring occasionally.

## BAKED POTATOES

Ingredients:

As many jacket potatoes you can fit in the crock pot

Olive oil

Directions:

Prick potatoes with fork and baste with olive oil so skins don't dry out.

Fill slow cooker with potatoes.

Cover and cook on high 1-2 hours or low 3-4 hours.

Do not add water.

If the potatoes are left too long in the crock pot they will change color meaning the sugars start to caramelize – they can still be eaten though.

## BANANA BREAD

Ingredients:

1 x ¾ c. flour (gluten-free or other)

2 tsp baking powder

¼ tsp baking soda

½ tsp salt

1/3 c. shortening

2/3 c. sugar (natural alternatives or leave out)

2 eggs, well beaten

1 ½ c. banana, well mashed, overripe

½ c. walnuts, coarsely chopped

Directions:

Sift together flour, baking powder, baking soda and salt.

With electric beater on low, fluff shortening in a small bowl, until soft and creamy.

Add sugar gradually if using.

Beat in eggs in a slow stream.

With a fork, beat in 1/3 of the flour mixture, ½ the bananas another 1/3 of the flour mixture, the rest of the bananas then the last of the flour mixture.

Fold in walnuts.

Turn into a greased and floured baking unit or a 2 ½ quart mold and cover.

Place on a rack in crock pot.

Cover crock pot, but prop the lid open with a toothpick or a twist of foil to let the excess steam escape.

Cook on high for 4 to 6 hours.

Cool on a rack for 10 minutes.

Serve Warm.

## BANANA NUT BREAD

Ingredients:

1/3 c. shortening

½ c. natural xylitol sugar

2 eggs

1- ¾ c. all purpose flour (you can use gluten-free like tapioca and gram flour)

1 tsp baking powder

½ tsp baking soda

½ tsp salt

1 c. mashed ripe bananas

½ c. chopped walnuts

Directions:

Cream together shortening and sugar.

Add eggs and beat well.

Sift dry ingredients.

Add to creamed mixture alternately with banana, blending well after each addition.

Stir in nuts.

Pour into well-greased ceramic souffle dish.

Cover with foil and tie a string tightly around it to keep foil down.

Pour 2 cups hot water in slow-cooking pot.

Place mold on rack or trivet in pot.

Cover with crock pot lid and cook on high 2 to 3 hours or until bread is done.

Be sure not to check bread during the first 2 hours of cooking.

## CAJUN PECANS

Ingredients:
1 pound pecan halves
4 tbsp butter, melted
1 tbsp chili powder
1 tsp salt
1 tsp dried basil
1 tsp dried oregano
1 tsp dried thyme
½ tsp onion powder
¼ tsp garlic powder
¼ tsp cayenne pepper

Directions:
Combine all ingredients in crock pot.
Cover and cook on high for 15 minutes.
Turn on low, uncovered, stirring occasionally for 2 hours.
Transfer nuts to a baking sheet and cool completely.

## CHUNKY APPLESAUCE

Ingredients:

8 to 10 large cooking apples, peeled, cored, and sliced or cut in chunks

½ cup water

1 tsp cinnamon

½ to 1 cup sugar

Directions:

Put ingredients in crock pot.

Cover.

Cook on low 8 to 10 hours. (High: 3 to 4 hours.)

Serve warm.

Add cream if desired.

## BREAKFAST CASSEROLE

Ingredients:

4 medium-sized apples, peeled and sliced

¼ cup honey

1 tsp. cinnamon

2 tbsp. butter, melted

2 cups granola cereal

Directions:

Place apples in slow cooker and mix in remaining ingredients.

Cover and cook on low for 7-9 hours (overnight).

Serve with milk.

# CRANAPPLE SAUCE

Ingredients:

10-12 medium apples

1-2 c. cranberry juice

lemon juice -- use 1/4 to 1/2 lemon

2 tbs natural sweetener (xylitol or stevia)

1/4 to 1/2 cup dried cranberries

Directions:

Wash the apples and chop them up without peeling.

Squeeze lemon juice over them as you cut them.

Put apples in crock pot with cranberry juice use 1 cup if you want the applesauce thick, more if you want it thin.

Stir in sugar to suit your taste.

Let apples stew on low for 6-8 hours.

About an hour or two before serving, stir in cranberries.

The applesauce is a very pretty pink and the cranberries & juice give it a nice zing.

As you can see, the recipe is simple and forgiving, let the apples stew a little longer or a little less, the longer you stew them the mushier the applesauce will be.

It warms up nicely, or you can eat it cold.

# Crock Pot Fish

## CITRUS FISH

Ingredients:
1 ½ lb. fish fillets
Salt and pepper to taste
1 med. onion, chopped
5 tbsp. chopped parsley
4 tsp oil
2 tsp grated lemon rind
2 tsp grated orange rind
Orange and lemon slices

Directions:
Butter crock pot and put salt and pepper on fish to taste.
Then place fish in pot.
Put onion, parsley and grated rinds and oil over fish.
Cover and cook on low for 1½ hours.
Serve garnished with orange and lemon slices.

## FISH IN TOMATO SAUCE

Ingredients:

4 x 6 oz (150g) white fish steaks or fillets

1 x 14 oz (400g) can organic peeled Italian plum tomatoes – chopped

1 tbsp organic tomato purée

minced or grated garlic – 2 cloves

fresh ground black pepper

salt to taste

1 diced green pepper

Directions:

Turn the crock pot onto low. Grease the inside.

Stir the tomato purée into the chopped tomatoes, season and add the green pepper and garlic

Put fish fillets in the bottom and pour over the tomato mixture.

Leave to cook for 3 to 5 hours - 2 to 3 hours on high if you prefer.

# Crock Pot Desserts

## APPLE CRANBERRY COMPOTE

Ingredients:

6 cooking apples, peeled, slice

1 cup fresh cranberries

1 cup sugar (xylitol)

½ teaspoons grated orange peel

½ cups water

¼ cups port wine

sour cream , (low fat)

Directions:

Arrange apple slices and cranberries in crock pot.

Sprinkle sugar over fruit.

Add orange peel, water and wine.

Stir to mix ingredients.

Cover, cook on low 4-6 hours, until apples are tender.

Serve warm fruits with the juices, topped with a dab of sour cream.

Serves 6.

## APPLE CRANBERRY CRISP

Ingredients:

3 apples (Any kind - I personally like Gala)

1 cup cranberries

¾ cup xylitol sugar or normal brown sugar if you haven't got xylitol

1/3 cup rolled oats (quick cooking)

¼ tsp. salt

1 tsp. cinnamon

1/3 cup butter, softened

Directions:

Peel, core and slice apples.

Place apple slices and cranberries in crock pot.

Mix remaining ingredients in separate bowl and sprinkle over top of apple and cranberries.

Place 4 or 5 paper towels over the top of the crock pot, place an object across the top of the crock pot and set lid on top.

This allows the steam to escape.

Turn crock pot on high and cook for about 2 hours.

Serves 4.

# BAKED APPLES

Ingredients:

6 lg. cooking apples

¾ c. orange juice

2 tsp. grated orange rind

1 tsp. lemon rind grated

¾ c. rose wine

¼ tsp. cinnamon

½ c. brown sugar optional – or xylitol or you could try honey

Whipped cream

Directions:

Remove core from apples and place in crock pot.

Mix together all other ingredients except whipped cream.

Pour over apples.

Cover pot and cook on low for about 3½ hours or until apples are tender.

Cool and serve with whipped cream.

## BREAKFAST COBBLER

Ingredients:

4 medium-sized apples -- peeled and sliced

¼ cup honey

1 tsp cinnamon

2 tablespoons butter -- melted

2 cups granola cereal

Directions:

Place apples in slow cooker and mix in remaining ingredients.

Cover and cook on low 7-9 hours (overnight) or on high 2-3 hours.

Serve with milk.

Yield: 4 servings

## CARROT PUDDING

Ingredients:

4 large carrots, cooked and grated

1 small onion, grated

½ teaspoon salt

¼ teaspoon nutmeg

1 tablespoon sugar (xylitol or honey)

1 cup milk

3 eggs, beaten

Directions:

Mix together carrots, onion, salt, nutmeg, sugar, milk, and eggs.

Pour into slow cooker and cook on high for 3-4 hours.

## CHRISTMAS BREAD PUDDING

Ingredients:

17 slices whole wheat bread or use some white bread as well

3 egg yolks, beaten

1½ cups light cream

2/3 cup dark Raisins

1/3 cup whole candied red cherries, halved

¾ cup cream sherry

1 cup - water

2 egg yolks, beaten

¼ cup Powdered Sugar, sifted

2 tablespoons Cream Sherry

1/3 cup sugar or sweet alternative eg. Stevia

dash salt

1 ½ teaspoons vanilla

2/3 cup golden raisins

¼ teaspoon vanilla

½ cup whipping cream

Directions:

Remove crusts from bread.

Cover bread slices with paper towels and let stand overnight.

**Custard:** in a heavy medium saucepan combine three egg yolks, light cream, sugar and salt.

Cook and stir over medium heat.

Continue cooking until mixture coats a metal spoon. Remove from heat; cool at once by setting saucepan in a sink of ice water and stirring for 1-2 minutes.

Stir in 1 ½ teaspoons vanilla.

Cover surface with clear plastic wrap. In small bowl combine raisins.

Place cherries in another bowl.

Heat ¾ cup sherry till warm.

Pour 2/3 cup sherry over cherries. Set aside. Cut bread into ½-inch cubes (about 9 cups).

In a bowl, fold bread into custard, until coated. Grease a 6 ½ cup tower mold (without tube).

Drain raisins and cherries, reserving sherry.

Arrange ¼ of cherries in bottom of the mold, sprinkle 1/3 cup raisins into the mold.

Add ¼ of bread cube mixture.

Sprinkle with 2 tablespoons reserved sherry.

Repeat layers three times, arranging cherries and raisins near edges of the mold.

Lightly press last layer with back of spoon.

Pour remaining reserved sherry over all.

Cover mold tightly with foil.

Set mold in cooker - for a 5-6qt cooker, pour 1½ cups water around mold (for a 3½ - 4 qt cooker use 1 cup water).

Cover, cook on low 5½ hours or until pudding springs back when touched.

Meanwhile make the sherry sauce: in a mixing bowl combine 2 egg yolks, powdered sugar, 2 tablespoons sherry and ¼ teaspoons vanilla.

In small bowl, beat whipping cream until small peaks form. Gently fold whip cream into egg yolk mixture.

Cover and chill until serving time.

Remove mold from cooker, let stand 10 minutes.

Carefully un-mold to serving platter.

Serve warm with sherry sauce.

Serves 12.

Alternative: Remove pudding from mold, cover and chill.

To serve, return pudding to same mold.

Cover with foil, place in cooker.

Pour 1½ cup water around mold.

Cover, cook on high for 1½ to 2 hours, or until warm. Let stand 10 minutes, un-mold and serve with sauce.

## APPLE SAUCE

Ingredients:

About 3 pounds apples, peeled, cored, and sliced

1/3 cup sugar (recommend - xylitol)

1 cinnamon stick

2 tbsp lemon juice

nutmeg

Directions:

Put apples in cooker, sprinkle with sugar and add cinnamon stick.

Sprinkle lemon juice on.

Cover and cook on low for 6½ to 8 hours til apples form a thick sauce.

Sprinkle with nutmeg to taste.

## Conclusion

I hope you have enjoyed the huge variety of dishes here. Invest in a good crock pot which will serve you many dinners and buy pots for freezing your meals so you can make a load and have at a later date.

If you are on a diet or want to lead a healthier lifestyle, I would like to recommend my other books which would certainly compliment this one – they are: *Green Smoothies & Other Healthy Smoothie Recipe* Book, *Fat Burning Foods* book and *Healthy Eating Tips* book.